PALABRA POR PALABRA

New Advanced Vocabulary

PHIL TURK

Hodder Murray

A MEMBER OF THE HODDER HEADLINE GROUP

Acknowledgements

I would like to thank the following for their comments, suggestions, typescript- and proof-reading and help in many other ways over the four editions of this book: Virginia Vinuesa Benítez, Derek and Loli Blake and their family, Mercedes Catton, Yvonne Chadwick, the late Antonio Moreno Carrascal, Susanne Elvira, José-Luis García Daza, Mike Zollo; also my wife, Brenda, for her customary patience and encouragement.

Although every effort has been made to ensure that website addresses are correct at time of going to press, Hodder Murray cannot be held responsible for the content of any website mentioned in this book. It is sometimes possible to find a relocated web page by typing in the address of the home page for a website in the URL window of your browser.

Hodder Headline's policy is to use papers that are natural, renewable and recyclable products and made from wood grown in sustainable forests. The logging and manufacturing processes are expected to conform to the environmental regulations of the country of origin.

Orders: please contact Bookpoint Ltd, 130 Milton Park, Abingdon, Oxon OX14 4SB. Telephone: (44) 01235 827720. Fax: (44) 01235 400454. Lines are open 9.00–5.00, Monday to Saturday, with a 24-hour message answering service. Visit our website at www.hoddereducation.co.uk

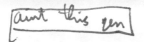

Introduction

This fourth edition of *Palabra por Palabra* has been extended with yet further words and phrases arranged by topic. Most of the chapters have been split into smaller, more manageable and more logically arranged sections, each numbered and with a sub-heading. Cross-references are provided where words relevant to a particular topic may be found in more than one chapter. Further words and phrases which have become current since the last edition have also been added, and a few which no longer seemed relevant have been discarded. Two new chapters have been added: Chapter 23, on false friends, and Chapter 24, containing a list of English words for which you need to be careful when finding equivalents in Spanish.

Some of the vocabulary is contextualised in short 'off-the-shelf' phrases, and can be used as such. You can also adapt them as necessary to fit other contexts. Many of the words and phrases have been taken from the Spanish press or the Internet and are therefore totally authentic. Others are the result of consultations with native Spanish speakers to find the equivalents of common phrases that occur in the English-speaking media.

The topics covered will be very useful for students tackling the AS and A2 specifications, as well as other students at a similar level of Spanish. Entries considered to be more suitable for A2 level or equivalent are indicated in bold type. At the end of most chapters you will find website addresses (both Spanish and Spanish American) which are a useful source for obtaining more information – and therefore more vocabulary – about aspects of the topic in question.

Learning vocabulary

As an advanced language student, you will by now be aware that words are the tools of the trade. However sound your knowledge of grammar and facts, and however brilliant your ideas, you cannot express them without the necessary words! And unlike when you learnt your mother tongue, unless you are very lucky, you won't be surrounded by people speaking Spanish all hours of your waking day. More likely your contact will be limited to a few hours of Spanish classes a week. Try, however, to increase your contact through websites, any newspapers, magazines or other materials in Spanish you can get hold of, your dictionary, and TV satellite programmes if you can receive them. We have provided you with a good selection of words and phrases on most of the topics you are likely to encounter, but you should also keep your own vocabulary notebook and jot down, as far as possible under topic headings, any further ones you come across.

Vocabulary learning is a very personal process and each of us will discover the method that suits us best. However, you must accept that it won't 'stick' without some effort on your part. The important thing is to experiment and find the method that works best for you! And, by the way, 'method' is the key word: you must be methodical! Try this…

- Find somewhere quiet: turn off that I-Pod!
- Decide which area of vocabulary you wish to concentrate on. (It should preferably be one you have been studying in class, so at least some of the words should be familiar, if not fully fixed in your mind!)
- Don't try to learn too much at once.
- By now you will probably have some idea how much you can absorb in one go: it's unlikely to be more than thirty words or phrases; it may be only twenty.
- Take the first ten words/phrases, read them through three times with the English.
- Cover the Spanish with a piece of paper and try the first one.
- Reveal the Spanish: did you get it right? If so, put a tick against it.
- Repeat for all ten words.
- Now take a further ten and repeat the process (and a further ten if your target is thirty).
- TAKE A BREAK.
- After that, come back to your vocabulary and repeat the process for each of the groups of ten words: put a second tick against each word you get right.
- Keep on repeating this process at intervals until you have at least three ticks against each word (five would guarantee a pretty foolproof imprint on your memory!).
- You can carry on these memory checks at odd moments during the day: just keep this book handy!
- Before you start on your next batch of about thirty, always check the previous thirty. You'll be surprised how the ticks mount up!
- When you come back to revise closer to your exam, repeat the process, adding a tick to each word you remember. Pay special attention to the words with fewer ticks!

You can also extend your vocabulary by taking a word and seeing how many related words you can find. For example, if you begin with *cocer* – to cook, you could add *cocción* – (process of) cooking, *cocido* – stew, *cocina* – kitchen, (skill of) cooking, cooker/stove, *cocinar* – to cook, *cocinero/a* – cook (person), etc. You could play this with a fellow student: each has to add a word. You can also do it with words associated by ideas: *cocina – gas – eléctrico – electricidad – luz – alumbrar* etc., or by opposites: *empezar–terminar*; *permitir–prohibir*.
And finally and most importantly: when you know these words, incorporate them into your work, whether it is written or spoken. Use them or lose them!

¡Suerte!
Phil Turk

Websites

There are a number of Spanish search engines, but I have not been able to put them all to the test. One that I have found reliable is www.terra.es, which is 'Google enhanced', and itself has a good list of immediate links (*enlaces*) relevant to several topics, without recourse to a search. However, you can perfectly successfully use well-known search engines such as Google and Yahoo by typing in www.google.es or www.yahoo.es, which will give you access to Spanish language websites.

General websites

All the main Spanish and Spanish American press publications have their own websites, with many features relevant to the topics covered in this book. The main ones are:

Newspapers:
El País: www.elpais.es
ABC: www.abc.es
El Mundo: www.elmundo.es
La Vanguardia: www.lavanguardia.es

Regional papers in the *Diario* series, e.g.:
Diario montañés (Cantabria):   www.eldiariomontanes.es

Magazines:
Cambio 16:   www.cambio16.info
Tiempo: www.tiempodehoy.com
Época: www.epoca.es
¡Hola!:   www.hola.com
Marca: www.marca.es

Other general websites with many useful links are the relevant Spanish government ministries:
Ministerio de Trabajo y Asuntos Sociales: www.mtas.es
Ministerio de Educación y Ciencia: www.mec.es
Ministerio de Industria, Turismo y Comercio: www.mityc.es
Ministerio de Agricultura, Pesca y Alimentación: www.mapya.es
Ministerio de Sanidad y Consumo: www.msc.es
Ministerio de Medio Ambiente: www.mma.es
Ministerio de Fomento: www.fomento.es

The country suffixes for Spanish American websites are:

Argentina:	.ar
Bolivia:	.bo
Chile:	.cl
Colombia:	.co
Costa Rica:	.cr
Ecuador:	.ec
Guatemala:	.gt
Mexico:	.mx
Nicaragua:	.ni
Panamá:	.pa
Paraguay:	.py
Perú:	.pe
El Salvador:	.sv
Uruguay:	.uy
Venezuela:	.ve

For example, the Peruvian Ministry of Education's site is: www.minedu.gob.pe

You will find a list of possible websites for further research at the end of most of the topic-orientated chapters in this book. Some of these are the websites of international organisations, e.g. the Red Cross (www.cruzroja.es), which will access the Spanish Red Cross.

¡Que te diviertas navegando!

Abbreviations

The following abbreviations are used in this book:

adj	adjective
adv	adverb
coll	colloquial
esp	especially
f	feminine
indic	indicative
inf	infinitive
intrans	intransitive
m	masculine
n	noun
pl	plural
pres	present
sb	somebody
sth	something
subj	subjunctive
trans	transitive
v	verb

Contents

1 Quiero decir...

The purpose of this section is to provide the vocabulary to enable you to state, develop and conclude a written or spoken argument. The subsections are arranged in an order that seems to be the most logical, but do remember that many words and expressions could well be used in other parts of the argument, and in other contexts.

1.1 Preparar el terreno — Preparing the ground

el tema	subject, topic, theme
el problema	problem
la crisis	crisis
la cuestión	question (for discussion)
primero	first, firstly
segundo	second, secondly
tercero	third, thirdly
en primer/segundo/tercer lugar	in the first/second/third place
al principio	at first, at the beginning
de antemano	beforehand
tenemos que preguntarnos	we have to ask ourselves
a primera vista	at first sight
a corto plazo	in the short term
a largo plazo	in the long term
ordenar los datos	to get the facts in order
despejar el terreno	to clear the ground
¿de qué se trata?	what is it about?
resumir el tema/la cuestión	to summarise the issue
afrontar el tema/la situación	to face (up to) the issue/situation
el problema que se plantea es...	the problem to be addressed/the problem that arises is...
es un tema que ya lleva varios años/meses apareciendo en los medios	it's a topic which has been in the media for several years/months now
es un tema que ya me preocupa/interesa desde hace algún tiempo	it's a topic that has been concerning/interesting me for some time now
será conveniente establecer los argumentos en pro y en contra	it will be useful to establish the arguments for and against
examinar más minuciosamente los argumentos	to examine the arguments in more detail

Handwritten annotations: EL, EL, LA; al principio; de antemano "other way of 'antes'"; a primera vista; a corto plazo; a largo plazo; resumir; afrontar

1

preocuparse = to worry

una crisis a escala mundial	a crisis on a world scale *inquietante*
una situación <u>inquietante</u>	a <u>worrying</u> situation *una s.. preocupante*
la <u>preocupación predominante</u>	<u>the main worry</u>

↳ *La preocupación predominante*

1.2 Aportar más ideas — Bringing in more ideas

<u>además</u>	besides, moreover
es más	moreover
además de lo dicho	in addition to what has been said
asimismo	likewise
en principio	in principle
en esto	at this point/stage
<u>por consiguiente</u> } <u>por consecuencia</u> }	consequently, therefore → *por* *consecuencia*
por otra parte	on the other hand
<u>debido a esto</u>	owing/due to this *debido a*
de hecho	in fact
dicho de otro modo	in other words
o sea...	or to put it another way..., or rather...
dicho eso	that said, having said that
no sólo... sino...	not only... but...
como ya se sabe	as we already know
es decir	that is to say, i.e.
en este contexto	in this context
por añadidura	in addition
a propósito	by the way
tanto... como...	both... and...
como resultado (de)	as a result (of)
resulta que...	it turns out that..., the result is that...
esto explica por qué...	this explains why...
no me explico por qué...	I don't understand why...
así	thus
así es que	therefore
por supuesto	of course
claro que (+ *clause*)	of course...
en realidad	in reality
aparte de eso	apart from that
se trata de	it's a question of

2

1.3 Obstáculos   Obstacles

pero	but
sin embargo	however
desgraciadamente ⎫ por desgracia ⎭	unfortunately
no obstante	nevertheless
a pesar de esto	in spite of this
el tropiezo	the stumbling block
sea como sea	be that as it may, that's as may be
la situación va empeorando	the situation is getting worse
teniendo en cuenta el hecho de que	bearing in mind the fact that
dado que	given that

1.4 Yo creo...   I think...

a mi parecer ⎫ a mi modo de ver ⎭	in my opinion
a mí me parece que... ⎫ yo opino que... ⎭	I think that...
por mi parte	for my part
desde mi punto de vista	from my point of view
(no) estoy de acuerdo con los que...	I am (not) in agreement with those who...
estoy persuadido/a de que (+ *indic*)	I am persuaded that...
no estoy persuadido/a de que (+ *subj*)	I am not persuaded that...
esto me lleva a pensar que...	this leads me to think that...
que yo sepa	as far as I know
yo que tú/usted	if I were you
no estoy totalmente a favor de (+ *n* or *inf*)	I'm not entirely in favour of
no estoy ni a favor ni en contra de (+ *n* or *inf*)	I'm neither for nor against
tengo que confesarme en contra de (+ *n* or *inf*)	I have to admit I am against
no es una opinión/actitud que comparta yo	it's not an opinion/attitude which I share
aunque quisiera pensar de otra manera	although I would like to think otherwise
tengo que confesarme partidario/a del comentarista	I have to confess to being on the side of the commentator

1.5 Otros dicen...   Others say...

hay quienes dicen que...	there are those who say that...
la gente piensa que...	people think that...
otros constatan que...	others maintain that...
la (gran) mayoría opina que...	the (vast) majority think that...
según se oye	according to what one hears
según una encuesta	according to a survey/opinion poll
sondar las opiniones	to sound out opinions
la verdad lisa y llana es...	the plain truth of the matter is...
cualquiera es capaz de ver que...	anyone can see that...
desde el punto de vista ajeno	from other people's point of view
es de presumir que... } según cabe presumir }	presumably
las cifras atestan que...	the figures prove that...
como ya se sabe	as is already known
que se sepa	as far as is known
no se puede menos de pensar que...	one cannot help thinking that...
es una ilusión creer que...(+ subj)	we're kidding ourselves if we believe that...
eso sería locamente optimista	that would be wildly optimistic
cualquiera que crea esto...	anyone who believes this...

1.6 La discusión sigue   The discussion continues

al contrario	on the contrary, on the other hand
visto así	seen like that
por un lado	on the one hand
por otro lado	on the other hand
de todos modos } de todas maneras/formas }	in any case, anyway
en lo que concierne } en cuanto a }	as for
en lugar de eso	instead of that
mientras que	whereas
no cabe duda de que...	there is no room for doubt that...
no se puede negar que...	there is no denying that...
es cierto que...	it's certain that...
lo esencial del caso (es que...)	the crux of the matter (is that...)
hay que tener en cuenta (que...)	you have to bear in mind (that...)
hay que subrayar la importancia de...	you have to emphasise the importance of...
se tiene que hacer hincapié en...	one has to make a special point of...
me limito a señalar	I limit myself to pointing out
más vale... que...	it's better to... than...

vale considerar...	it's worth considering...
según toda probabilidad	in all probability
nadie ignora que...	everybody knows that, nobody is unaware that...
por si acaso	just in case
no hay manera de saber si...	there is no way of knowing whether...
para colmo	to cap it all
y por si eso fuera poco	and as if that were not enough
no hay manera de saber si...	there is no way of knowing whether...
a juzgar por...	to judge by..., judging by...
en función de...	in proportion to..., according to (in that sense)...
en razón de...	by reason of..., because of..., due to...

1.7 Por ejemplo   For example

consideremos	let's consider
pongamos por caso lo de...	let's take for example the matter of...
en concreto	in particular
según el caso	as the case may be
para ilustrar el problema	to illustrate the problem
con respecto a...	with regard to...
vamos a abordar otro aspecto	let us tackle another aspect
para considerar el asunto más detalladamente	in order to consider the matter in more detail
vamos a profundizar	let us think about it in greater depth
vale agregar que...	it's worth adding that...

1.8 ¿Cómo?   How?

¿hasta qué punto?	to what extent?
hasta cierto punto	to a certain extent
extremadamente	extremely
totalmente	completely, utterly
principalmente	mainly, principally
tanto más	all the more so
de cierto modo de cierta manera/forma	in a certain way
de ningún modo de ninguna manera	in no way
de un modo u otro de una manera u otra	in one way or another
apenas	hardly

en ninguna circunstancia	in no circumstance(s)
simplemente } sencillamente	simply
puramente	purely, merely
prácticamente	practically, nearly
parcialmente	partially, partly
igualmente	equally, to the same extent
efectivamente	actually, in fact
parecido a... } similar a...	like..., similar to...
por la mayor parte	for the most part, mostly
a cambio de...	in exchange for...
sin más ni más	without further ado
se trata de saber cómo...	it's a question of knowing how...

1.9 ¿Cuándo?   When?

durante estos últimos años/meses	in the last few years/months
hace poco	a short time/while ago
anteriormente	formerly
recientemente	recently
recién construido	recently/newly built
recién nacido	recently/newly born
(recién *can be used with various past participles in this sense*)	
en el momento que...	at the moment when...
en aquel mismo momento	at that very moment
en un momento dado	at a given moment
hoy (en) día	nowadays
en la actualidad	nowadays, at the present time
la situación actual	the present/current situation
mientras tanto	meanwhile, in the meantime
de antemano	beforehand, in advance
posteriormente } con posterioridad	subsequently, afterwards
cuanto antes } lo más pronto posible	as soon as possible
dentro de unos pocos días	in a few days' time
dentro de poco	soon, in a short time
sin demora	without delay
algún día	some day
desde ahora	from now (on)
a partir de este/ese momento	from this/that moment (on)
a continuación	then, next, below (on page or in list)
desde...hasta...	from...until...
nunca más	never again
en la Edad Media	in the Middle Ages

en la época de la dictadura	at the time of the dictatorship
la década	decade
durante los años noventa	during the (19)90s
al final del siglo	at the turn of the century
tardar (mucho/largo) tiempo en + *inf*	to take a (very) long time in (doing)
cada cuando	every so often
cada pocos días	every few days
a cualquiera hora	at any time
por primera/segunda/última vez	for the first/second/last time
por enésima vez	for the umpteenth time
cada vez (que…)	each/every time (that…)

1.10 ¿Por qué? Why?

preguntarse por qué	to wonder why
deberíamos preguntarnos si…	we should ask ourselves if/ whether…
según los datos	according to the facts
eso explica por qué…	that explains why…
no me explico por qué…	I can't explain why…
se trata de saber por qué…	it's a question of knowing why…
debemos tratar de descubrir por qué…	we must try to find out why…
¿para qué?	what for?, for what purpose?
para comprender mejor	in order to understand better
para que comprendamos mejor	in order/so that we can understand better
puesto que… } ya que… }	since/because…
por cualquier razón	for whatever reason
la razón principal	the main reason
la piedra clave	the keystone, the keynote

1.11 La verdad es que… The truth is that…

The expressions followed by que *in this section all express fact or assumed fact, and are therefore followed by the indicative.*

claro que es verdad que…	of course it's true that…
lo cierto es que…	what is certain is that…
no cabe duda de que…	there's no doubt that…
en efecto yo diría que…	in fact I'd say that…
quiero dejar muy claro que…	I want to make it very clear that…
el caso es que…	the fact is that…

otro factor es que...	another factor is that...
no se puede negar que...	it cannot be denied that...
queda innegable que...	it remains/is undeniable that...
es de suponer que...	one presumes/supposes that...
parece ser que...	it seems that...
debemos tener en cuenta que...	we have to bear in mind that...
si nos damos cuenta de que...	if we realise that...
resulta que...	the result is/it turns out that...
de ahí que...	that's the reason why...
el dilema es que...	the dilemma is that...
actualmente se calcula que...	at the moment it is estimated/ calculated that...
un 70% de los entrevistados opina que...	70% of those interviewed reckon that...
hay quienes afirman que...	there are those who maintain that...
estar consciente de que...	to be conscious/aware that...
menos mal que...	it's a good job/thank goodness that...

1.12 Mi juicio es que... My judgement is that...

When the phrase makes a judgement or indicates a purpose, the verb which follows que *is in the subjunctive. Remember that the tense of the subjunctive will depend on the rules of tense sequence, and therefore phrases containing* sería, *which is conditional, would require the imperfect subjunctive. These are marked with an asterisk (*).*

a mí me parece lógico que...	it seems logical/sensible to me that...
no me sorprende que...	I'm not surprised that...
todo esto justifica que...	all this justifies (the fact) that...
parece inverosímil que...	it seems unlikely that...
parece mentira que...	it seems incredible that...
a mí me resulta curioso que...	I find it extraordinary that...
más vale que...	it's better/best that...
a mí no me importa que...	it's of no concern to me/it doesn't matter to me whether/that...
no es porque...	it's not because...
¿no parece significativo que...?	doesn't it seem significant that...?
esto explica que...	this explains why...
hay que asegurar que...	one has to ensure that...
es intolerable/insoportable que...	it's intolerable that...
me preocupa bastante que...	I'm somewhat worried that...
¿por qué tenemos que soportar que...?	why should we put up with the fact that...?

sería un milagro que...*	it would be a miracle if...
mi preferencia sería que...*	my preference would be that...
¿no sería mejor que...?*	wouldn't it be better if...?
si no fuera porque*...	if it weren't for the fact that...
es de suma importancia que...	it is of extreme importance that...
¿por qué no exigimos todos que...?	why doesn't everyone demand that...?
es de lamentar que...	it is to be regretted that...
es una vergüenza nacional que...	it's a national disgrace that...
es una afrenta a la sociedad que...	it's an affront to society that...
es incluso más sorprendente que...	it's even more astonishing that...
tiene que ser inconcebible que...	it has to be unthinkable that...
lo fundamental debe ser que...	the main thing should be that...
pongamos por caso que...	let us suppose that...

1.13 La validez del argumento / The validity of the argument

razonar	to reason
el razonamiento	the reasoning
un caso irrecusable	a watertight case
un argumento robusto	a strong/robust argument
este modo de enfocar la cuestión	this approach to the question
si aceptamos este enfoque	if we accept this approach/line of argument
el argumento no vale, porque...	the argument is no good, because...
rechazar un argumento	to reject an argument
condenar rotundamente	to condemn roundly
ver/no ver lo esencial del asunto	to see/miss the point
el argumento no está bien fundado	the argument won't hold water
no tiene pies ni cabeza	it's all at sixes and sevens
carece de sentido	it lacks sense/meaning
carece de sustancia	it lacks substance
el punto flaco del argumento	the weak point of the argument
no tiene nada que ver con la realidad	it has nothing to do with reality
hacer la vista gorda (a)	to turn a blind eye (to)
pongamos el argumento patas arriba	let's turn the argument on its head

1.14 Soluciones y conclusiones Solutions and conclusions

de acuerdo	agreed
(estar) de acuerdo con...	(to be) in agreement with
¡vale! (*coll*)	right!
a fin de cuentas	after all, when all is said and done
en resumen	to sum up (*adv*), in brief
resumir	to sum up
la clave del problema tiene que ser	the key to the problem has to be
la solución que se destaca	the solution which stands out
tomar medidas urgentes	to take urgent measures
para que la situación siga mejorando	so that the situation continues to improve
de modo que la situación no empeore	so that the situation does not deteriorate
vuelvo a mi primera observación	I return to my first statement
ya hemos constatado que...	we have already stated that...
volvamos al punto de partida	let us return to the starting point
teniendo en cuenta todos los puntos de vista	bearing in mind all points of view
podemos deducir que...	we can deduce that...
es una perspectiva optimista	the outlook is optimistic/bright
poco optimista	not very optimistic
(muy) pesimista	(very) pessimistic/ gloomy
(nada) favorable	(not very) favourable
aunque con ciertas dudas/reservas	although with certain doubts/ reservations
por fin	finally, at last
en conclusión ⎫ para concluir ⎭	in conclusion
esto nos lleva a la conclusión inevitable (que...)	this brings us to the inevitable conclusion (that...)
ojalá pudiera concluir diciendo que...	I wish I could conclude by saying that...
no hay otra conclusión que valga	there is no other valid conclusion

2 La gente: la personalidad y el carácter

The words and phrases in this chapter do not belong to any particular examination topic, but might be applied to any real or fictitious persons under any topic heading. You might well find them useful in describing family members in Chapter 3 and film, drama or literary characters associated with Chapter 22.

la cualidad	quality
el rasgo la característica }	feature, trait, characteristic
característico (*adj*) de	characteristic of
típico (de)	typical (of)
la virtud	virtue
la preferencia	preference
el estado de ánimo	**mood, frame of mind**
relacionarse con alguien	**to relate to sb**
tratar con alguien	**to have dealings with sb**

2.1 Las cualidades positivas   Positive qualities

llevarse bien con alguien	to get on well with someone
tener el don de...	to have the gift of...
tener sentido del humor	to have a sense of humour
conservar la calma	to keep calm, keep one's cool
reflexionar antes de actuar	**to think before acting**
tomarse la vida tal como viene	**to take life as it comes**
actuar por instinto	**to act instinctively**
estar bien dotado de sentido común	**to be well endowed with common sense**
ser abierto/a	to be open, of an open disposition
ser alegre	to be happy, jolly (i.e. visibly that sort of person)
ser amistoso/a ser amigable }	to be friendly
ser atento/a	to be thoughtful, kind
ser autosuficiente	to be self-sufficient
ser bondadoso/a	to be kind, generous
ser cariñoso/a	to be affectionate, loving, tender

11

cariño/a	darling, dear
ser cauto/a	to be cautious, wary
ser convencional	to be conventional
ser chistoso/a	to be funny, witty
ser agudo/a ⎫ ser diestro/a ⎭	to be skilful, clever
ser exigente	to be demanding
ser autoexigente	to expect a lot of oneself
ser extrovertido/a	to be an extrovert
ser feliz	to be happy (by nature)
la felicidad	happiness
ser honrado/a	to be honest
la honradez	honesty
ser imaginativo/a	to be imaginative
<u>ser</u> listo/a	to be <u>clever</u>
<u>estar</u> listo/a	to be <u>ready</u>
ser luchador(a)	to be a fighter
ser maduro/a	to be mature
la madurez	maturity
<u>ser</u> optimista	to be <u>an optimist</u> (by nature)
<u>estar</u> optimista	to be <u>optimistic</u> (about something)
ser perceptivo/a	to be perceptive
ser perfeccionista	to be a perfectionist
ser persistente	to be persistent
ser risueño/a	to be cheerful, of a sunny disposition
ser sensible	to be sensitive (NOT sensible)
la sensibilidad	sensitivity
ser sincero/a	to be sincere
la sinceridad	sincerity
ser tolerante	to be tolerant
la tolerancia	tolerance

2.2 Los rasgos negativos   Negative features

la obsesión	obsession
obsesionarse por...	**to be obsessed with...**
la fobia	phobia
no poder soportar	not to be able to put up with
el defecto	defect
estar en un constante estado de...	to be in a constant state of...
tener una tendencia a...	to have a tendency to...
odiar	to hate
el odio	hate, hatred
despreciar	to scorn, disdain
el desprecio	scorn, disdain
volverse irritable	to get irritable

sentirse algo inseguro/a	to feel a bit insecure
ver con malos ojos	**to take a dim view of**
no ver más allá de las narices	**not to see further than one's nose**
tener mal genio	**to be bad-tempered, of an evil disposition**
estar lleno/a de contradicciones	**to be full of contradictions**
lucirse	**to show off**
hacer autobombo	**to blow one's own trumpet**
ser apático/a	to be apathetic
ser asqueroso/a	to be revolting, disgusting
ser brusco/a	to be abrupt, sharp, rude
ser canalla	to be a swine, a rotter
ser conflictivo/a	to be argumentative, quarrelsome
ser camorrista ⎫ ser chismoso/a ⎭	to be a gossip
los chismes	gossip, tittle-tattle
no ser honrado/a	to be dishonest
la falta de honradez	dishonesty
ser egoísta	to be selfish
ser emotivo/a	to be emotive, emotional
dejarse arrastrar por las emociones	**to let oneself be ruled by one's emotions**
ser encogido/a ⎫ ser tímido/a ⎭	to be timid, shy
ser envidioso/a	to be envious
ser engreído/a	to be conceited
ser fantasioso/a (*coll*)	to be conceited, stuck up
ser gruñón/gruñona	to be grumpy (by nature)
ser imbécil	to be an idiot
<u>ser</u> indeciso/a	to be <u>indecisive</u> (by disposition)
<u>estar</u> indeciso/a	to be <u>undecided</u> (at this moment)
ser introvertido/a	to be an introvert
ser malévolo/a	to be malicious, spiteful
ser mezquino/a	to be mean, stingy
ser miedoso/a	to be timid, nervous
<u>ser</u> pesimista	to be <u>a pessimist</u> (by nature)
<u>estar</u> pesimista	to be <u>pessimistic</u> (about something)
ser posesivo/a	to be possessive
ser rebelde	to be unruly, rebellious
ser superficial	to be superficial
ser supersticioso	to be superstitious
ser terco/a	to be stubborn, obstinate
ser testarudo/a	to be stubborn, pigheaded
ser torpe	to be clumsy, awkward, dull, dim
ser vago/a	to be slack, lazy
ser vengativo/a	to be spiteful, vindictive
ser vergonzoso/a	to be shy, timid

3 La gente: la familia y las relaciones personales

You will know the Spanish for most of your close family members by now, but here is a reminder that when used in the masculine plural, the word often means 'one of each sex':

los padres	parents
los tíos	uncle and aunt
los abuelos	grandparents

La familia y los familiares — Family and relatives

los familiares	relatives
los parientes	relatives (NOT parents!)
el/la cuñado/a	brother/sister-in-law
el/la hermanastro/a	stepbrother/stepsister
la madrastra	stepmother
la nuera	daughter-in-law
el padrastro	stepfather
el/la primo/a	cousin
el/la sobrino/a	nephew/niece
los sobrinos	nephews and nieces
el/la suegro/a	father/mother-in-law
el yerno	son-in-law
el árbol genealógico	family tree

3.1 Las relaciones en general — Relationships in general

hacerse amigo/a de alguien	to become somebody's friend
la amistad	friendship
entablar amistades	to strike up friendships
el desarrollo de la personalidad	the development of the personality
llevarse bien/mal con...	to get on well/badly with...
tener una relación especial con...	to have a special relationship with...
confiar en los amigos	to confide in/trust one's friends
compartir/guardar un secreto	to share/keep a secret
respetar los sentimientos ajenos	to respect other people's feelings
tolerar a los demás	to tolerate others

sentir alegría ante el bien ajeno	to feel joy at others' wellbeing
armar un follón	to cause a row, to kick up a fuss

3.2 El amor   Love

el/la novio/a	boyfriend/girlfriend
ligar con un chico/una chica	to go out with/date a boy/girl
el ligue (*coll*)	boyfriend
sentirse atraído/a por...	to feel attracted by/to...
enamorarse	to fall in love
estar enamorado/a (de)	to be in love (with)
el amor a primera vista ⎫	love at first sight
el flechazo ⎭	
estar chiflado/a por alguien	to be crazy about sb
llevar una relación seria	to carry on a serious relationship
evolucionar una relación	**to evolve/work out a relationship**
flirtear/coquetear con alguien	to flirt with sb
enrollarse con alguien	to chat sb up
el cariño	affection
cariñoso/a	affectionate
hacer el amor	to make love
sentir celos	to feel jealous
dar calabazas a alguien	to jilt sb
la orientación sexual	sexual orientation
del sexo opuesto	of the opposite sex
del mismo sexo	of the same sex
una relación heterosexual/	a heterosexual/homosexual
homosexual	relationship
la homosexualidad	homosexuality
el lesbianismo	lesbianism
ser gay/lesbiana	to be gay/lesbian

3.3 Vamos a casarnos   Let's get married

el/la prometido/a	fiancé(e)
prometerse (con)	to get engaged (to)
estar prometido/a/os	to be engaged
el noviazgo	engagement
la pareja	couple
prometer	to promise
casarse (con)	to get married (to)
la boda	wedding (i.e. the ceremony)
el casamiento	wedding/marriage (ceremony
	or state)

el matrimonio	marriage (the state)
contraer matrimonio	to enter into matrimony/marriage
la dama de honor	bridesmaid
el padrino de boda	best man
el anillo	ring
el voto	vow
estar felizmente casados	to be happily married
ayudarse uno a otro	to help each other
el apoyo mutuo	mutual support
ser/quedarse soltero/a	to be/remain single

3.4 La familia y los niños   Family and children

los padres | los progenitores	parents
estar embarazada	to be pregnant
quedar embarazada	to get pregnant
parir	to give birth (to)
el parto	birth (in sense of delivery)
nacer	to be born
el/la bebé | el/la nene/a	baby
la criatura	baby, small child
los gemelos	twins
tienen tres críos	they've got three kids
la niñera	childminder, nanny
la baja de maternidad/paternidad	**maternity/paternity leave**
el cochecito de niño	pram
la sillita de ruedas	pushchair
cambiar los pañales a un bebé	to change a baby's nappy
el/la protector(a)	guardian
el/la canguro	baby-sitter
hacer/estar de canguro	to baby-sit
el/la hijo/a mayor	the elder/eldest son/daughter
el/la menor	the youngest
el benjamín	the youngest son
el padrino	godfather
la madrina	godmother
los padrinos	godparents
el cumpleaños	birthday
cuando Pedro cumplió siete años	when Pedro was (i.e. reached) seven years old
el santo	saint's day
el bautizo	christening, baptism
bautizar	to christen, baptise

se le puso Miguel	he was christened/baptised Miguel
el nombre (de pila)	name (first/Christian name)
la maternidad	maternity
la paternidad	parenthood, fatherhood
amamantar	to suckle, breastfeed
dar el pecho	to breastfeed
la cuna	cradle
mecer	to rock

criar una familia	to bring up/raise a family
la infancia	infancy
el jardín de infancia	kindergarten
la guardería (infantil)	nursery, crèche
los recuerdos de la niñez	childhood memories
la canción infantil	nursery rhyme
desde niño/a	from childhood
de niño/a	as a child

mimar a un niño	to spoil a child
una familia unida	a close family
monopolizar el cariño de los padres	to monopolise parents' affection
en el seno de la familia	in the heart of/within the family
mostrar autoridad	to show authority
crear lazos de afecto	to create bonds of affection
evitar favoritismos	to avoid favouritism
crear un estrecho vínculo	to create a close bond

el maltrato a los niños	child abuse

3.5 La vida sexual   Sex life

la planificación familiar	family planning
la contracepción/anticoncepción	contraception
la píldora anticonceptiva	contraceptive pill
los métodos anticonceptivos	contraceptive methods, birth control methods

el anticonceptivo	contraceptive
el preservativo/el condón	condom
el control de la natalidad	birth control
dejar embarazada a una mujer	to get a woman pregnant
un embarazo (no) deseado	a wanted (an unwanted) pregnancy
interrumpir el embarazo	to terminate pregnancy
el feto	foetus
el ciclo menstrual	menstrual cycle
el aborto	abortion

abortar	to have an abortion/a miscarriage
fecundar	to fertilise
la hormona	hormone
concebir	to conceive
la fecundación in vitro	in vitro fertilisation
el niño probeta	test-tube baby
la inseminación artificial	artificial insemination
la madre portadora	surrogate mother

3.6 El divorcio — Divorce

divorciarse	to get divorced
estar divorciado/a	to be divorced
solicitar un divorcio	to apply for a divorce
la tasa de divorcio	the divorce rate
la orientación matrimonial	marriage guidance
el consejero de orientación matrimonial	marriage guidance counsellor
iniciar los procedimientos del divorcio	to initiate divorce proceedings
el alejamiento	estrangement
convivir	to live together
un proceso penoso	a painful process
la ruptura matrimonial	marriage break-up
ser incompatibles	to be incompatible
cuando un matrimonio se deshace	when a marriage breaks up
la separación	separation
separarse	to become separated
perjudicar gravemente	to prejudice seriously
hijos, bienes y posesiones	children, property and possessions
el padre soltero	single father/parent (male)
la madre soltera	single mother/parent (female)
el custodio de los niños	custody of the children
el/la cónyuge	spouse
andar en relaciones con	to have an affair with
la infidelidad	infidelity
volver a casarse	to remarry

3.7 La mujer — Women

el feminismo	feminism
los derechos de la mujer	women's rights
los malos tratos	ill-treatment, abuse

(no) tratar a la mujer como **objeto sexual**	(not) to treat women as sex objects
objeto de deseo	objects of desire
como si fuera algo normal	as if it were something normal
cuidar de la casa y de la familia	to look after the house and family
'en casa y con la pata quebrada'	'at home and with her leg broken' (old Spanish proverb, suggesting the woman's place is in the home – even if you have to break her leg to keep her there!)
la publicidad machista	male-orientated advertising
el papel de la educación es primordial	**the role of education is of prime importance**

You will find more useful vocabulary concerning women at work in Chapter 6.

3.8 La tercera edad   Senior citizens

jubilarse	to retire
estar jubilado/a	to be retired
los jubilados	retired people
el/la pensionista	pensioner
la persona de la tercera edad	senior citizen
la libreta de pensión	**pension book**
el plan de pensiones	**pension scheme**
la vida empieza a los 60 años	life begins at 60
el abono para la tercera edad	**pensioners' travel pass**
para las personas de 65 años o más	for people of 65 and over
para los mayores de 65 años	
hacer lo que te dé la gana	**to do as you please**
el asilo de ancianos	old people's home
geriátrico/a	geriatric
estar postrado/a en cama	**to be bedridden**
el servicio de comidas a domicilio	**meals on wheels**
tener que depender de otros	**to have to depend on others**

www.mujeractual.com/familia
www.familia.cl
www.terceraedad.org

4 Los jóvenes

la adolescencia	adolescence
(el/la) adolescente	adolescent (*n* or *adj*)
de niño/a	as a child, when X was a child
ir creciendo	to be growing up
el comportamiento	behaviour
comportarse	to behave

4.1 Los problemas de hacerse adulto
Problems of growing up

el estado de ánimo	state of mind
estar en la edad del pavo	to be at the awkward age
estar en la edad de querer independizarse	to be of an age to want one's independence
le cuesta mucho concentrarse	he/she finds it difficult to concentrate
estar hecho/a un lío	to be all mixed up
deprimirse	to get depressed
sentirse deprimido/a	to feel depressed
el estado de depresión	state of depression
cabrearse (*coll*)	to get mad, livid
amargar	to make bitter
amargarse	to feel/become bitter
sentir amargura	to feel bitterness
sentirse amargo/a	to feel bitter
estar harto/a (de)	to be fed up (with)
hartarse (de)	to get fed up (with), weary (of)
el desarrollo de la personalidad	the development of the personality
tener problemas al relacionarse con la gente	to have problems relating to people
contar mentirillas	to tell lies, fibs
encontrarse inseguro/a	to feel insecure
superarse a sí mismo	**to take oneself in hand, control oneself**
sentir la necesidad de ser uno mismo	**to feel the need to be oneself**

4.2 Las relaciones con los padres

Relations with parents

la autoridad	authority
las actitudes	attitudes
cuestionar la autoridad	to question/challenge authority
la autoridad paterna	parental authority
rebelarse contra la autoridad	to rebel against authority
la permisividad paterna	parental permissiveness
los padres indulgentes	lenient, tolerant parents
castigar	to punish
las reglillas	petty rules
el comportamiento antisocial	antisocial behaviour
soltar palabrotas	to swear, use bad language
mostrarse mal educado/a	to make a show of bad manners
montar/armar un follón	to cause a row, kick up a fuss
reñir	to quarrel
ponerlo todo en tela de juicio	**to question everything**
llegar de madrugada	to come home in the small hours
querer salirse con la suya	to want to get one's own way
no poder entenderse con su padre/madre	to be unable to get on with one's father/mother
su madre es una antigualla	**his/her mother is old-fashioned**
su padre es un chapado a la antigua	**his/her father is an old fuddy-duddy**
estar estrecho/a de miras	**to be narrow-minded**
mis padres insisten en que yo (+ subj)	**my parents insist that I...**
fastidiar a alguien	to get on someone's nerves
buscar cinco pies al gato	**to make a lot of fuss over nothing, exaggerate**
escuchar todos los días el mismo rollo	to hear the same old thing day after day
como si fuese lo único que importase	**as if it were the only thing that mattered**
no tener prejuicios	**to be open-minded**
compartir ideas	to share ideas
no importa quién tiene razón	it doesn't matter who's right
no es porque no lo intente	**it isn't for want of trying**

hacer las paces	to make it up
cada cual ofrece su opinión	each one offers his/her opinion
ponerse de acuerdo	to reach an agreement
estar de acuerdo	to be in agreement, agree

4.3 El desafecto juvenil — Disaffection of young people

4.3.1 Las causas — Causes

el desencanto	disenchantment, disillusion(ment)
la falta de oportunidades	lack of opportunities
las frustraciones	frustrations
sentirse perseguido/a y acosado/a	to feel persecuted and harassed
sentirse/estar marginado/a	to feel/be marginalised
la presión del grupo paritario	peer group pressure
no integrarse en el tejido social	to remain outside the social fabric
apurar el instante	to live for the moment
desperdiciar la juventud	to squander one's youth
necesitar una dosis de aventura	to need a dose of adventure
romper la aplastante rutina social	to break the soul-destroying daily routine
vivir el presente	to live for the present

4.3.2 Las manifestaciones — The signs

la agresividad	aggressiveness
asumir una actitud provocativa	to adopt a provocative attitude
la crispación	tension
destrozarlo todo	to smash everything up
los enfrentamientos	confrontations
(bajo) los efectos del alcohol o de la droga	(under) the influence of drink or drugs
entonarse	to get high
hacerse el chulo	to act big/smart
el hurto	theft
lanzar improperios	to hurl abuse
las luchas callejeras	street fights
montar bronca	to cause a riot
el movimiento punk	the punk movement
no soportar el aspecto de alguien	not to be able to stand someone's appearance
usar el argot callejero	to use street slang

4.3.3 Puntos de vista

Points of view

no se puede soportar este modo de comportarse	we can't put up with this sort of behaviour
a mí no me extraña que haya tanta violencia	I'm not surprised that there's so much violence

4.3.4 Los tipos

Types

el/la drogodelincuente	drug-addicted criminal
la pandilla	gang
la tribu	tribe
la guerra tribal	tribal warfare, gang warfare
los grupos organizados de fanáticos	organised groups of fanatics

4.3.5 El fútbol

Football

la violencia futbolística	football violence
una orgía de violencia	an orgy of violence
desatar la violencia	to unleash violence
la bomba de humo	smoke bomb
el petardo	firecracker
el hincha ⎱ el forofo (*coll*) ⎰	fan, supporter
la prohibición de vender alcohol	ban on the sale of alcohol

4.3.6 Soluciones

Solutions

mantener el orden	to keep order
un fenómeno creciente	a growing phenomenon
la protección policial	police protection

4.4 La música pop

Pop music

la canción	song
grabar en disco	to record
la letra	lyrics, words (of a song)
el pinchadiscos	disc-jockey, DJ
la estrella de pop	pop star
la gira por Estados Unidos	US tour
el concierto	gig, concert
el festival pop	pop festival
las listas de éxitos	the charts
el disco número uno	number one hit
el sistema de amplificación	PA system
los amplificadores	loudspeakers, amplifiers

el teclado	keyboard
tocar la batería	to play the drums
los palillos	drumsticks
tocar la guitarra eléctrica	to play the electric guitar
el sintetizador	synthesiser
el/la solista	lead (singer/player)
doblar	to dub
las luces estroboscópicas	strobe lights
los focos	lights
los fans	fans

4.5 La moda — Fashion

la creación original	original creation
dar una buena imagen	to give a good image
el/la diseñador(a)	designer
el/la modisto/a	fashion designer
la manera de vestirse	way of dressing
lucir un nuevo vestido	to show off a new dress
la preocupación por vestir bien	the desire to be well-dressed
la caída de la chaqueta	**the hang of a jacket**
tener un buen aspecto	to look good
los vuelos de la falda	the spread/swirl of a skirt
saber elegir lo más elegante	**to know how to choose the smartest (clothes, etc.)**
saber cómo vestir	to know how to dress, have good dress sense
vestirse de una manera estrafalaria	**to dress outlandishly**
vestirse al estilo punk	to dress in punk style
lucir una cazadora de cuero negro	to sport a black leather bomber jacket
los vaqueros rotos	ripped jeans

www.injuve.mtas.es
www.cje.org
www.cruzrojajuventud.org

5 La enseñanza

la escuela	school (usually primary)
el colegio (el cole)	state primary school or private school, all ages up to 18
el instituto	state secondary school (12–18)
el centro	centre (often used just to denote school)
la asignatura	subject
la vuelta al cole/colegio	back to school
el/la profesor(a)	teacher
el/la profe (coll)	teacher
el/la maestro/a	primary teacher
el castigo	punishment
castigar	to punish

5.1 La escolaridad   The school system

el centro docente	educational/teaching establishment
Educación Básica Obligatoria	compulsory basic education
Educación Primaria	primary education
Educación Secundaria Obligatoria	compulsory secondary education
el módulo	module
el instituto	state secondary school (12–18)
el internado	boarding school
la academia	'crammer'
el parvulario	play school, kindergarten
un traslado de colegio	a change of school
el curso	school year
pasar de curso	to move up a year
la escolaridad	period of schooling, school system
matricularse	to sign on, to enrol (for a school)
el rendimiento escolar	school performance
las clases particulares	private classes
los métodos de enseñanza	educational/teaching methods
el folleto de información	information booklet
el temario	syllabus
las materias obligatorias	compulsory subjects
las instalaciones deportivas	sports facilities
mandar partes a casa	to send a report home
la parte de clase	school report

5.2 Tus capacidades y aptitudes

Your capabilites and aptitudes

un método infalible	an infallible method
el/la alumno/a talentoso/a	gifted pupil
estar bien motivado/a	to be well motivated
me falta la motivación	I lack motivation
me cuesta concentrarme	I find it hard to concentrate
la capacidad de trabajo	capacity for work
tener la sed de conocimientos	to have a thirst for knowledge
hacer un mayor esfuerzo	to make a greater effort
devanarse los sesos	to rack one's brains

las asignaturas que presentan mayor dificultad	the subjects which present the greatest difficulty
abordar primero las asignaturas difíciles	**to tackle the difficult subjects first**
las asignaturas que se pueden superar con más facilidad	**the subjects which can be most easily mastered**
tener aptitud para los idiomas	to have a flair for languages
no soy muy bueno/a en ciencias	I'm not very good at science
ser empollón/empollona (*coll*)	to be a swot
ser curroadicto/a (*coll*)	to be a workaholic
(no) vale el esfuerzo	it's (not) worth the effort
¡ya caigo!	got it!
¡no caigo!	I don't get it!

organizar su tiempo	to organise one's time
obtener resultados	to obtain results
conocer sus deficiencias	to know one's weaknesses
la capacidad de retener	**the ability to retain knowledge**
perder el hábito del estudio	**to get out of the habit of studying**
un sistema adecuado a las capacidades y aptitudes del alumno	**a system suited to the capabilities and aptitudes of the pupil**
desarrollar la capacidad autocrítica	**to develop one's capacity for self-appraisal**

5.3 Los problemas escolares Problems at school

el fracaso escolar	failure at school
fracasar	to fail, to be a failure (in school)
la falta de escolaridad	lack of schooling
las expectativas de los progenitores	parents' expectations
la sobreexigencia	over-expectation
flojear/ser flojo/a (en)	to be weak (at)
la escasa atención de los padres	lack of parental attention
la dislexia	dyslexia
ser disléxico/a	to be dyslexic
sufrir retraso escolar	to fall behind in one's schooling
repetir curso	to repeat a year
faltar a clase	to skip lessons
la masificación en las aulas	overcrowding in the classrooms
los materiales trasnochados	out-of-date materials
garantizar/mejorar la calidad en enseñanza	to guarantee/improve the quality of education

5.4 Las oportunidades Opportunities

la igualdad de oportunidades	equality of opportunities
ampliar la formación	to broaden one's education
moldear las generaciones futuras	to shape future generations
la política educativa del gobierno	government education policy
la natalidad de los años noventa	the birth rate in the nineties
el gasto estatal en educación	state expenditure on education
proceder de las clases sociales más desfavorecidas	to come from the most disadvantaged social classes

5.5 El personal docente Teaching staff

hacer oposiciones para profesor(a)	to apply for a teaching job
enseñar una asignatura	to teach a subject
dar clase a los alumnos	to teach pupils
el/la principal	headteacher, principal
el/la pedagogo/a	pedagogue, 'posh' word for teacher
el/la catedrático/a	head of department/faculty
el/la agregado/a	assistant teacher
el/la PNN (penene) = profesor(a) no numerario/a	probationary or trainee teacher

el/la bedel(a)	caretaker, head porter
el claustro	**staff meeting**
las cualidades del profesor	a teacher's attributes
mantener la disciplina	to maintain discipline
relacionarse con los alumnos	to relate to one's pupils
no tener favoritismos	not to have favourites
ser capaz de motivar a los alumnos	to be capable of motivating pupils
esforzarse en hacer las clases más agradables	to try to make classes more enjoyable
autoritario/a	authoritarian
poco exigente	undemanding, lax
relajado/a	relaxed, laid back
austero/a	austere
estricto/a	strict
fomentar la discusión	to encourage discussion
reciclarse	to retrain
los profesores reclaman su valoración en la sociedad	**teachers demand to be appreciated in society**

5.6 Los exámenes — Examinations

la evaluación	assessment (test held several times during the school year in Spanish schools)
sacar buenas/malas notas	to get good/bad marks
sacar un sobresaliente	to get an 'excellent'
un notable	a 'very good'
un bien	a 'good'
un suficiente	a 'satisfactory'
un insuficiente	an 'unsatisfactory'
un muy deficiente	a 'very poor'
aprobar un examen por los pelos	to scrape through an exam
suspender un examen	to fail an exam
la recuperación	retake
la chuleta (coll)	'crib'
salir preparado para poder incorporarse al mercado de trabajo	**to come out ready and able to be absorbed into the labour market**

28

5.7 La universidad — University

el sistema universitario	the university system
acceder a la enseñanza universitaria	to gain access to university education
ingresar en la universidad	to get into university
la solicitud de admisión	entry application
la selectividad	university entrance exams
lograr títulos	to get qualifications
el procedimiento de selección	selection procedure
cursar estudios universitarios	to follow a university course
la facultad universitaria	university faculty
el intercambio de conocimientos	exchange of knowledge
la libre circulación de las ideas	free circulation of ideas
una experiencia enriquecedora	**an enriching experience**
el enriquecimiento	**enrichment**
el desarrollo cultural/científico/ tecnológico	cultural/scientific/technological development
la convalidación mutua de títulos	**mutually agreed validation of qualifications (between countries)**
las humanidades	arts, humanities
las ciencias	sciences
la licenciatura	degree
ser licenciado/a de derecho	to have a degree in law
las tasas	tuition fees
conseguir una beca	to get a grant
el préstamo gubernamental	government loan
reembolsar un préstamo	to repay a loan
estar pelado/a	to be hard up
estar sin blanca	to be strapped for cash, 'skint'
la tesis doctoral	doctoral thesis
la fuga de cerebros	brain drain
las manifestaciones estudiantiles	student demonstrations
el líder estudiantil	student leader

www.mec.es
www.me.gov.ar
www.sep.gob.mx

6 El trabajo

el comercio	business, commerce, business studies
el/la director(a)	director, manager
la ambición	ambition
la compañía	company, firm
la empresa	company, firm
cobrar	to earn
ganar	to earn
la experiencia laboral	work experience
el/la aprendiz(a)	apprentice
el aprendizaje	apprenticeship
tomar un año libre	to take a gap year/year off
la formación profesional	vocational training

6.1 La carrera — Career

6.1.1 Solicitar trabajo — Applying for jobs

andar en busca de empleo	to be on the lookout for a job
solicitar un puesto de trabajo	to apply for a job
el anuncio	advertisement
leer en las 'ofertas de trabajo'	to read in the 'Situations Vacant'
responder a un anuncio	to reply to an advert
la agencia de colocaciones	employment agency
el INEM (Instituto Nacional de Emplco)	Ministry of Employment, (also equivalent of) government job centre
hacer oposiciones	to seek a job by public competition (mainly in Spanish Civil Service)
se necesita fontanero	vacancy for a plumber
un trabajo muy solicitado	a much sought-after job
la hoja de solicitud	application form
escribir una carta de solicitud	to write a letter of application
me permito dirigirme a usted para (+ *inf*)	I am writing to you in order to ...
el curriculum vitae	curriculum vitae, CV
los datos personales	personal data
los títulos académicos	academic qualifications
con licenciatura en ...	with a degree in ...

la experiencia profesional	professional/work experience
pedir informes/referencias	to ask for references
dar informes/referencias	to give references, act as referee
en respuesta a su anuncio publicado en...	in reply to your advertisement published in ...
las aficiones	interests
tengo un año de experiencia en ...	I have a year's experience in ...
aunque no tengo experiencia en ...	although I have no experience in ...
tengo el dominio del español	I speak very good Spanish
ofrecer mis servicios como ...	to offer my services as ...
la entrevista	interview
entrevistarse bien	to interview well
ir bien vestido/a	to be well/smartly dressed
ser apto/a para el trabajo	to be suitable for the job
incorporarse al trabajo lo antes posible	**to go out to work as soon as possible**
conseguir un trabajo por enchufe	**to get a job through connections, by pulling strings**
estar bien enchufado/a	**to have good connections, be well connected**
me ofrecieron el trabajo	I was offered the job
me rechazaron	they turned me down
el rechazo	rejection, refusal
rechacé el puesto	I turned the job down

6.1.2 Las ambiciones   Ambitions

ser ambicioso/a	to be ambitious
mi única ambición es hacerme...	my one ambition is to become a...
le falta ambición	he/she has no ambition
buscarse una carrera en la informática	to seek a career in information technology
planificar su futuro	to plan one's future
apuntar alto	to aim high
poner las miras en un puesto alto	to set one's sights on a top job
sacar adelante la carrera	to foster/advance one's career
aspirar a periodista	to have aspirations to be a journalist
prepararse para fontanero	to train as a plumber
seguir un curso de ingeniería	to follow a course in engineering
hacer un aprendizaje en carpintería	to do a carpentry apprenticeship
estudiar para abogado	to study to become a lawyer
soñar con hacerse estrella de cine	to dream of becoming a film star
trabajar de camarero	to work as a waiter
hay que promocionar la imagen	**one needs to promote one's image**
el potencial adquisitivo	**earnings potential**

6.2 El personal — Staff, personnel

un puesto de alta dirección	a senior management position
el/la director(a) general	managing director
el/la director(a) de ventas	sales manager
el/la director(a) de personal	personnel manager
los altos cargos	**top people**
la oficina central	head office
el/la secretario/a de dirección	management secretary
el/la empresario/a	manager/boss
el/la encargado/a	foreman/woman
la plantilla	staff
la mano de obra	workforce
el/la empleado/a de banco	bank employee
el/la obrero/a	worker
el/la funcionario/a	civil servant
el/la empleado/a	employee
el/la trabajador(a)	worker
el peón	unskilled worker
el peonaje	unskilled workforce, labourers
el trabajador eventual	casual worker
el jornalero	piece worker
un trabajo de cuello blanco	a white-collar job
ser trabajador(a) autónomo/a	to be self-employed
experimentado/a	experienced
generar empleo	to generate employment
cambiar de empleo	to change jobs
la satisfacción en el trabajo	job satisfaction
el estatus	status

6.3 Las condiciones del trabajo — Working conditions

el mercado de trabajo	**the labour market**
la rentabilidad	**profitability**
la productividad	**productivity**
la competencia	**competition**
la creación de empleo	**creation of employment**
el contrato	**contract**
contratar	**to contract, take on**
un trabajo especializado	**a specialised job**
el sector de servicios	**the service sector**

la banca	banking
el sucursal	branch
la población obrera	the working population
el trabajo a pleno tiempo	full-time work
el trabajo a tiempo parcial	part-time work
el trabajo a destajo	piecework
el trabajo a tiempo flexible } **la flexibilización de horarios** }	flexitime
el trabajo por turnos	shiftwork
trabajar horas extra	to work overtime
el pluriempleo	having more than one job
asalariado	waged, salaried
el salario mínimo	minimum wage
el sueldo	pay, salary
las posibilidades de promoción	promotion possibilities
las normas de seguridad	safety regulations
sentirse a gusto en el trabajo	to like one's work
el absentismo	absenteeism

6.4 La mujer en el trabajo   Women at work

la incorporación de la mujer en el trabajo	the involvement/acceptance of women at work
la discriminación sexual	sex discrimination
la igualdad de oportunidad	equality of opportunity
cobrar el 30 por ciento menos	to earn 30% less
estar peor pagadas que los hombres	to be worse paid than men
pocas ocupan los altos cargos	few occupy the top jobs
el acoso sexual	sexual harassment
acosar	to harass
una cuestión de actitudes	a question of attitudes
la guardería	crèche
el horario flexible	flexible hours
el permiso por maternidad	maternity leave
poder diversificar su elección profesional	to be able to vary one's choice of job
tener que sacar adelante el trabajo de fuera y dentro de la casa	to have to work outside and inside the home
la necesidad de compaginar la vida familiar con la profesional	the need to reconcile family and professional life

You will find further vocabulary on the subject of women in Chapter 3.

6.5 En la oficina | In the office

6.5.1 La correspondencia comercial | Business correspondence

Note: in business correspondence, if you are writing to and/or on behalf of your company, you tend to use the plural; if you are writing to a particular person representing that company, use the singular. Unless you are very well acquainted with your addressee(s) you will normally use usted/ustedes.

Muy señor mío	Dear Sir (person to person)
Muy señora mía	Dear Madam (person to person)
Muy señores nuestros	Dear Sirs (from firm to firm)
Estimado Sr. Ramírez	Dear Mr Ramírez
Estimada Sra. Blas	Dear Mrs Blas
acuso/acusamos recibo de su carta del 12 de abril	thank you for your letter of 12th April
con referencia a su pedido del 8 de mayo	with regard to your order of 8th May
en respuesta a su anuncio en *El Diario*	in reply to your advertisement in *El Diario*
tenemos el gusto de informarles que...	we have pleasure in informing you that...
hemos recibido una solicitud de información sobre ...	we have received a request for information about...
le(s) agradecería/agradeceríamos nos mandara...	I/we would be grateful if you would send us...
tenga(n) la bondad de comunicarnos su respuesta lo antes posible	please reply as soon as possible
tenga(n) la bondad de responder por fax/correo electrónico/por vuelta de correo	please reply by fax/email/ return of post
de acuerdo con sus instrucciones	in accordance with your instructions
adjunto encontrará(n)...	please find enclosed...
le/la saluda atentamente	yours faithfully (from one person)
les saludan atentamente	yours faithfully (from company)

NB if in doubt, you can just say atentamente!

remitente/rte.	sender (on back of envelope)
impresos	printed matter
certificado	registered (mail)
confidencial	confidential

6.5.2 Al teléfono   On the phone

telefonear/llamar por teléfono	to phone
la llamada telefónica/el telefonazo	phone call
¿me pone con la centralita?	can you put me through to the switchboard?
¿de parte de quién?	who's calling?
está(n) comunicando	the line is engaged
¿podría llamarme más tarde?	could he/she/you phone me later?

6.5.3 El trabajo secretarial   Old-style secretarial work
a la antigua

These words are included in case you should need them. You will find the main vocabulary associated with communications and information technology on pages 107–109 and business and finance on pages 101–103.

el/la secretario/a	secretary
la máquina de escribir	typewriter
escribir un documento a máquina	to type a document
el teclado	keyboard
el procesador de textos	word processor
archivar	to file
el/la taquígrafo/a	shorthand writer
tomar taquigráficamente	to take down in shorthand
el fichero	filing cabinet

6.6 Las relaciones laborales Labour relations

el sindicato	trade union
el sindicalismo	trade unionism
el sindicalista	trade unionist
el enlace sindical	shop steward
la solidaridad de la clase obrera	working-class solidarity
el/la representante	representative
la tasa de inflación	the inflation rate
la reducción de la jornada de trabajo	reduction in the working day
exigir retribuciones mejores	**to demand better remuneration**
las vacaciones retribuidas/pagadas	**paid holidays**
el coste de la mano de obra	**labour costs**
el derecho a la huelga	the right to strike
ponerse en huelga ⎫	to go on strike
ir a la huelga ⎭	

la comisión	committee
el convenio colectivo	collective agreement
la convocatoria	strike call
convocar manifestaciones	to call demonstrations
reivindicar	to claim, demand
la reivindicación	claim, demand
la huelga salvaje	wildcat strike
la huelga de solidaridad	sympathy strike
imponer un período de enfriamiento	to impose a cooling-off period
las negociaciones	negotiations
cuarenta horas semanales	forty-hour week
despedir por razones disciplinarias	to dismiss, sack on disciplinary grounds
la flexibilización de horarios	flexitime
negociar	to negotiate
la subida de salario	salary/wage increase
yo creo que hay otras formas de protestar y conseguir lo que se pide	I think there are other ways of protesting and achieving one's demands
la huelga es el método más eficaz con el que cuenta la gente para que la escuchen	striking is the most effective way to get people to listen to you
no se consiguió nada con la huelga	the strike achieved nothing

6.7 El paro — Unemployment

6.7.1 El sistema — The system

el paro } el desempleo }	unemployment
estar parado/a } estar desempleado/a }	to be unemployed
el paro a largo plazo	long-term unemployment
las cifras/la tasa del paro/desempleo	the unemployment figures
los costes salariales	wage costs
el subsidio	benefit
el subsidio de paro/desempleo	dole
despedir	to sack, fire, dismiss
despedir temporalmente	to lay off
el despido	redundancy
la compensación por despido	redundancy pay

la reducción de la plantilla	reduction in staff
reducir la plantilla sin despedir	to reduce staff by natural wastage
obligar a una persona a que se jubile anticipadamente	to force someone into early retirement

6.7.2 Las consecuencias   The consequences

estar parado/a, desempleado/a	to be unemployed
los parados/desempleados	the unemployed
incorporarse a las colas de los parados	to join the dole queues
sentirse rechazado/a	to feel rejected
sentirse sin valor	to feel worthless
los resultados psicológicos de estar parado/a	the psychological results of being unemployed
ser una estadística	to be a statistic
reciclar a alguien	to retrain sb
reciclarse	to retrain (i.e. to get retrained)
el reciclaje	retraining
dimitir	to resign, take voluntary redundancy
jubilarse	to retire
adaptarse a los cambios	to adapt to changes
acostumbrarse a los cambios tecnológicos	to get used to technological changes

www.mtas.es/mujer
www.inem.es

7 El ocio

la actividad	activity
el aficionado	fan
el atletismo	athletics
el asiento	seat
el baile	dance
bailar	to dance
el baloncesto	basketball
el boxeo	boxing
el/la cantante	singer
la ciencia-ficción	science fiction
el concierto	concert
la corrida de toros	bullfight
el deporte	sport
el/la deportista	sportsman/woman
deportivo/a	sports (adj), sporting
la diversión	entertainment, amusement
divertirse	to enjoy oneself
¡que te diviertas!	enjoy yourself, have a good time!
la entrada	(entry) ticket
el equipo	team
el espectáculo	show
el esquí	ski, skiing
esquiar	to ski
el estadio	stadium
la función	function
el hobby	hobby
el interés	interest
el/la jugador(a)	player
nadar	to swim
la natación	swimming
participar (en)	to take part (in)
el partido	game, match
el pasatiempo	hobby, pastime
el polideportivo	sports centre
los ratos libres ⎫ el tiempo libre ⎭	free/spare time
la sala de fiestas	hall
la taquilla	box office
tocar un instrumento	to play an instrument
el videojuego	videogame

7.1 Los deportes — Sports

las actividades lúdicas	recreational activities
ser deportivo/a	to be keen on sport
las instalaciones deportivas	sports facilities
la selección	team (selection)
la plantilla	squad
la junta directiva	**management committee**
los seleccionadores	the selectors
el liderazgo	leadership
el/la entrenador(a)	trainer
entrenarse	to train
el/la adversario/a	opponent
el/la árbitro/a	referee, umpire
el terreno de juego	the field of play
el vestuario	changing room
el campeonato	championship
el campeonato mundial	world championship
la Liga	league
la copa	cup
el trofeo	trophy
derrotar	to defeat
la derrota	defeat
permanecer imbatido/a	to remain unbeaten
la competición	competition (contest or act of competing)
los deportes competitivos	competitive sports
el concurso	competition (= contest)
la competencia	competition (= competitiveness)
el deporte de equipo	team sport
el equipo rival	the rival team
el espíritu de rivalidad	rivalry, competitive spirit
el espíritu de equipo	team spirit
el/la vencedor(a)	the winner
el resultado	result
coger la iniciativa	to take the initiative
jugar bien bajo presión	to play well under pressure
patrocinar	to sponsor
el/la patrocinador(a)	sponsor
el grupo patrocinador	sponsoring group
el patrocinio	sponsorship

7.1.1 El fútbol y el rugby   Football and rugby

la temporada de fútbol	football season
el abono de temporada	season ticket
los delanteros	forwards
los defensores	defence
el ariete	striker
el enfrentamiento	encounter, confrontation
la fase final del campeonato	the final phase of the championship
marcar un gol	to score a goal
lograr el primer gol	to achieve the first goal
hacer circular el balón	to pass the ball around
chutar	to shoot
la mano	handball (i.e. touching with hand)
ceder un penálty	to give away a penalty
la quiniela (futbolística)	football pools
el boleto	pools form
el ensayo	try
el drop	drop goal
transformar	to convert
las competiciones europeas	European competitions
el partido tendrá lugar	the match will take place
el torneo	tournament
marcar un ensayo	to score a try
ganar cinco puntos	to win/score five points
¿cómo van?	what's the score? (game in progress)
¿cuál es el resultado?	what's the (final) score/result?
el Real Madrid batió al Barcelona de dos a uno	Real Madrid beat Barcelona 2–1
empatar con...	to draw with...
el resultado fue empate cero a cero	the result/score was a nil-nil draw

7.1.2 El atletismo   Athletics

el/la atleta	athlete
el/la corredor(a)	runner, competitor, athlete
batir el record	to beat the record
la carrera	race
los cien metros lisos	the hundred metres flat
el maratón	marathon
el salto de longitud/de altura	long/high jump

los Juegos Olímpicos	Olympic Games
la Olimpiada	Olympiad
el estadio olímpico	Olympic stadium
conseguir una medalla de oro/plata/bronce	to get a gold/silver/bronze medal
la ciudad anfitriona	host city
las pruebas	trials

7.1.3 Otras actividades deportivas

Other sporting activities

el tenis	tennis
el golpe	shot
el revés	backhand
la volea	volley
el saque	service
la pista de tenis	tennis court
pasarse los sábados en el campo de golf	to spend one's Saturdays on the golf course
el patinaje sobre hielo	ice skating
la pista de patinaje	skating rink
el campeón/la campeona internacional sobre hielo	international ice champion
el patinaje artístico	figure skating
entusiasmarse por el esquí	to be mad on skiing
las pistas de esquí	ski slopes
dedicarse al ciclismo	to do a lot of cycling
la vuelta a España	cycle race around Spain, 'tour d'Espagne'
las carreras de caballos	horse racing
el hipódromo	racecourse
apostar	to bet
jugarse el dinero	to gamble
el juego de azar	game of chance
cazar	to hunt, shoot
ir a la caza	to go hunting/shooting

los deportes con un alto componente de riesgo	high-risk sports
bucear	to skin-dive
el buceo	skin-diving
el traje isotérmico	wetsuit
el vuelo libre	hang gliding
el ala (f) delta	hang glider
el ultraligero	microlight
despegar	to take off
aterrizar	to land
la pista de aterrizaje	runway, landing strip
pertenecer a un club de deportes acuáticos	to belong to a water sports club
acceder a un cursillo de iniciación	**to go on a beginner's course**
el senderismo	hiking, trekking
salir de excursión	to go on a trip
la ornitología	ornithology, bird watching
ser amante del aire libre	to be fond of the fresh air
costearse el equipo	to afford the equipment
los gastos de mantenimiento	maintenance costs

7.1.4 Juegos y pasatiempos de salón / Indoor games and pastimes

un pasatiempo terapeútico	a therapeutic pastime
dedicarse al coleccionismo	to go in for collecting
coleccionar sellos/monedas	to collect stamps/coins
ampliar su colección	to expand one's collection
reunir las antigüedades	to collect antiques
el afán de guardar	**the urge to hoard things**
atesorar	to treasure
tener valor sentimental/como curiosidad	to have sentimental/curiosity value
ir haciéndose con objetos	**to go on acquiring things**
tener una auténtica pasión de coleccionista	**to have a real passion for collecting**
la obra de arte	work of art
la tienda especializada	specialist shop
sacar fotos/fotografías	to take photos
revelar un rollo de película	to develop a roll of film
la cámara digital	digital camera
la tarjeta de memoria	memory card
imprimir	to print
rechazar	to reject
borrar	to erase

¿te apetece una partida de ajedrez?	do you fancy a game of chess?
la tabla/pieza de ajedrez	chess board/piece
dar mate (a algiuen)	to checkmate (sb)
asistir a una clase nocturna	to go to an evening class
empezar con el español	to take up Spanish
no hacer nada en absoluto	to do nothing whatever
echarse una siestecita	to have forty winks/a snooze
no mover un dedo para ayudar en la cocina	**not to lift a finger to help in the kitchen**
quedarse pegado/a al televisor	to be glued to the television
pasarse los ratos libres escuchando CDs/su MP3	to spend one's free time listening to CDs/one's MP3

7.2 La comida y la bebida   Eating and drinking

7.2.1 Comer   Eating

la cocina española	Spanish cooking
ser cocinero/a experto/a	to be an expert cook
los comestibles	foodstuffs
saborear un plato	to savour, taste a dish
saber a ajo	to taste of garlic
picante	hot (spicy)
el menú gastronómico	gourmet menu
el menú turístico	cheap, set menu
el plato combinado	set main course
ser goloso/a	to have a sweet tooth
ser glotón/glotona	to be a glutton
salir al restaurante	to eat out
el restaurante de cinco tenedores	'five fork' (= luxury) restaurant
tomarse unos pinchos/unas tapas	to have some 'tapas'
ofrecer un ambiente acogedor	to offer a friendly atmosphere
no es un restaurante cualquiera	it's not any old restaurant
se come bien ahí	the food's good there
la comida rápida	fast food
la hamburguesería	burger bar

7.2.2 Beber | Drinking

vamos a tomar algo	let's have a drink
el refresco	soft drink
la bodega	wine bar
la denominación de origen	mark of origin (of wine)
el vino corriente/el peleón	ordinary wine, 'plonk'
la fiesta	party
el club nocturno	night club
la juerga	binge
emborracharse	to get drunk
estar borracho como una cuba	to be as drunk as a lord
ser borracho	to be a drunkard
cogerse una borrachera	to go on a drinking binge
la litrona	2-litre bottle of beer
hacer un botellón	to drink a lot of alcohol in public places, to go binge drinking
ir de bares	to go on a pub-crawl
la resaca	hangover
abstenerse	to abstain
abstenerse del alcohol ⎱ ser abstemio/a ⎰	to be teetotal
las bebidas sin alcohol	non-alcoholic drinks
someter a la prueba del alcoholímetro	to breathalyse

You will find further leisure activities in Chapter 22.

http://es.sports.yahoo.com
www.marca.es

8 La vida urbana

la acera	pavement
las afueras	suburbs, outskirts
aparcar	to park
el aparcamiento	car park
la avenida	avenue
el barrio	district, suburb
la calle	street
céntrico/a	central
el centro comercial	shopping centre/mall
concurrido/a	busy (crowded)
la fábrica	factory
el/la habitante	inhabitant
la zona	district, area

8.1 La administración y los habitantes — Administration and inhabitants

el/la ciudadano/a	citizen, town dweller
el/la madrileño/a	citizen of Madrid
el/la barcelonés/esa	Barcelona
el/la sevillano/a	Seville
el ambiente	ambience, atmosphere
la capital administrativa	administrative capital
la capital económica	economic capital
el municipio	town, municipality, town council
el Ayuntamiento	town hall, town council
el concejo	council
el/la concejal(a) municipal	town councillor
la Diputación	equivalent of District Council
el presupuesto comunitario	the community budget
la urbanización	urban development
la planificación urbana	town planning

8.2 El tráfico y el transporte urbano

Traffic and urban transport

8.2.1 La infraestructura

Infrastructure

el casco histórico	historic centre
el barrio antiguo	old quarter
el paso elevado	flyover
el paso subterráneo	underpass
la peatonalización	pedestrianisation
crear más zonas peatonales	to create more pedestrian areas
la autopista elevada	elevated motorway
la autovía	dual carriageway
la glorieta	roundabout
la carretera de circunvalación	ring road
la necesidad de más variantes	**the need for more bypasses**
la calle de dirección única	one-way street
la desviación	diversion
el carril de bus	bus lane
el cruce de peatones	pedestrian crossing
la pista para ciclistas	cycle track/lane
volver a descubrir la bicicleta	to rediscover the bicycle
el lobby ciclista	the cycling lobby
el aparcamiento subterráneo	underground carpark
no se puede estacionar/aparcar	you can't park
estacionamiento prohibido	no parking
la multa	fine
multar	to fine
el/la guardia de tráfico	traffic policeman/woman, traffic warden
el semáforo estaba en rojo	the traffic lights were red
calle cerrada por obras	street closed for roadworks
la grúa	crane (to tow away cars)
remolcar	to tow (away)
el cepo	wheelclamp
la remodelación del centro	**redevelopment/restructuring of city centre**
la vigilancia policial	police patrol
una solución al tráfico de Madrid	a solution for the Madrid traffic

8.2.2 Los transportes públicos

Public transport

aprovechar los transportes públicos	to make use of public transport
el abono	travel card
el descuento	discount
el usuario de los autobuses	bus user
los autobuses van hasta los topes	the buses are packed

8.2.3 La congestión

Congestion

la(s) hora(s) punta	rush hour, peak time
el caos del tráfico	traffic chaos
el atasco	traffic hold-up
atascarse	to be held up
el tráfico rodado	wheeled traffic
el embotellamiento	traffic jam, bottleneck
agravar el problema del tráfico	to worsen the traffic problem
el tráfico es desesperante	the traffic is impossible

8.2.4 Las condiciones ambientales

Environmental conditions

el ruido infernal	infernal noise
el humo de los tubos de escape	exhaust fumes
emitir gases nocivos	to emit noxious fumes
causar problemas respiratorios	to cause respiratory problems
el circulo vicioso	vicious circle
la polución/la contaminación	pollution
polucionar/contaminar	to pollute/contaminate
hacer estragos con la salud	**to wreak havoc with one's health**
el viajero diario/la viajera diaria	commuter
viajar diariamente al trabajo	to commute to work

You will find further vocabulary on the subject of transport in Chapter 10, and on the environment in Chapter 14.

8.3 La vivienda   Where people live

las condiciones de vivienda	living conditions
la aglomeración	conurbation
la ciudad dormitorio	dormitory town
la vecindad	neighbourhood
los vecinos	neighbours
la manzana	block (of buildings)
el inmueble de lujo	luxury property
el rascacielos	skyscraper
el chalé	detached house
la agencia inmobiliaria	estate agent's
el piso piloto	show flat
el bloque de pisos	block of flats
con cocina amueblada	with a fitted kitchen
el/la propietario/a	owner, proprietor
el/la inquilino/a	tenant
el domicilio	address, home
una casa de alquiler	a rented house
alquilar un piso	to rent a flat
arrendar	to rent
deber el alquiler	to owe the rent
la vivienda	dwelling
la hipoteca	mortgage
hipotecar	to mortgage
la vivienda unifamiliar	**one-family dwelling/unit**
la casucha	**hovel**
la chabola	**hovel, shanty**
el barrio de chabolas	**shanty town**
los sin hogar	homeless people
dormir al descubierto	to sleep rough
el barrio desfavorecido	**run-down district**
el espacio verde	green space
la residencia secundaria	second home
el polígono residencial	residential development, estate
dar prioridad a la estética	**to give priority to aesthetic considerations**
el solar de construcción	**building site**
modernizar	to modernise
reparar	to repair
derribar/derrumbar	to demolish, pull down
derribarse/derrumbarse	to collapse
descuidar un edificio	to neglect a building
descuidado	run-down

en las afueras	on the outskirts
en el casco urbano	in the city centre
el almacén	store (shop or warehouse)
la gran superficie ⎱ el hipermercado ⎰	hypermarket
los grandes almacenes	department store(s)
la zona industrial	industrial zone/park
el polígono industrial	industrial estate

8.4 La seguridad ciudadana   Public safety

la inseguridad ciudadana	citizens' feeling of insecurity/ decline in law and order
el atraco	assault, mugging
atracar	to assault, mug
mejorar el alumbramiento público	to improve street lighting
la farola	street light
los problemas de los barrios céntricos	inner-city problems
un problema con pocas vías de solución	an almost insoluble problem
mendigar	to beg
el/la mendigo/a	beggar
la mendicidad	begging
el vagabundo	tramp
el squatter	squatter
la depravación urbana	urban deprivation
los vigilantes	vigilantes
la autodefensa	self-defence
la vigilancia vecinal	neighbourhood watch
la policía de barrio	neighbourhood police
la oferta de viviendas disponibles	building stock
la escasez de viviendas	housing shortage
la necesidad de viviendas	housing needs
el programa de vivienda	housing programme
la escasez de viviendas de alquiler	shortage of rented property

 www.dgt.es

49

9 La vida rural

9.1 La tierra — The land

el campo	the country (as opposed to town)/ arable field
el/la campesino/a	peasant, countryman/woman
el terreno	plot
tener 20 hectáreas de terreno	to have 20 hectares of land
la parcela	small plot, strip of land
parcelar	to divide into small plots
depender de la agricultura	to depend on agriculture
no se puede vivir de la tierra	you can't live off the land
la huerta	market garden
la finca	property, country estate
la granja	farm (usually small, in northern Spain)
el cortijo	farm, estate (especially in Andalucía)
el minifundio	**smallholding, small farm**
el latifundio	**large estate**
el minifundista	**smallholder**
el latifundista	**owner of large estate**
el minifundismo/latifundismo	**ownership corresponding to the above, often with reference to problems caused by the respective systems**
el terrateniente ausente	**absentee landlord**
heredar una parcela	**to inherit a plot**
la reforma agraria	**agrarian/land reform**
integrarse en una cooperativa	**to join/form a cooperative**
convertirse en ciudad dormitorio	**to become a dormitory town**

9.2 La agricultura   Agriculture

9.2.1 La labranza de la tierra   Working the land

el/la agricultor(a)	farmer
la zona agrícola	agricultural/farming area
el pueblo agrícola	farming village
arable	arable
cultivar patatas	to grow potatoes
los cultivos	crops
los productos	produce, crops
el cultivo de naranjas	orange growing
el/la cultivador(a) de aceitunas	olive grower
el/la aceitunero/a	olive picker
la recolección de la aceituna	olive gathering
la cosecha	harvest, crop
la cosechadora	combine harvester
cosechar a máquina	to harvest by machine
la mecanización de la agricultura	mechanisation of agriculture
coger a mano	to pick by hand
segar	to reap
la siega	reaping
arar la tierra	to plough (up) the land
el arado	plough
el surco	furrow
germinar	to germinate
irrigar	to irrigate
regar	to water, irrigate
la acequia	irrigation channel
el desagüe	drain, outlet
los cereales	cereals
sembrar trigo	to sow wheat

NB: *Rather than use a general word for 'field' such as* campo, *Spanish often adds* -al *to the crop grown, hence:*

el trigo/el trigal	wheat/wheatfield
el maíz/el maizal	maize/maize field
la cebada/el cebadal	barley/barleyfield
el arroz/el arrozal	rice/rice field, paddy field
la berza/el berzal	cabbage/cabbage field etc
la naranja/el naranjal	orange/orange grove

Note also:

la cañavera/ el cañaveral	reed grass/reed grass bed(s), > Cabo Cañaveral = Cape Canaveral, where the USA launches its space vessels!
el olivo	olive tree
el olivar	olive grove
las verduras	greens, vegetables
las hortalizas	vegetables, garden produce
la necesidad de modernizar la agricultura	the need to modernise agriculture
el programa de modernización agrícola	agricultural modernisation programme
el invernadero	greenhouse
cultivar bajo plástico	to grow under plastic
el cultivo orgánico	organic farming
favorecer abonos químicos/ orgánicos	to favour chemical/ organic fertilisers
los nitratos calan la tierra	nitrates soak into the soil
el estiércol	manure
la tierra baldía	sterile, waste land
dejar en barbecho	to leave fallow, set aside
la subvención agrícola	farm subsidy
la Política Agraria Común (PAC)	Common Agricultural Policy (CAP)

9.2.2 La cría del ganado y otros animales
Rearing cattle and other animals

la ganadería ⎫	stockbreeding, cattle raising,
la industria ganadera ⎭	cattle farming
el ganado	stock, livestock
el/la ganadero/a	stockbreeder, cattle raiser
la feria de ganado	cattle fair
el novillo	bullock, steer
el vaquero	herdsman, cowman
el prado/la pradera	meadow, grazing land
pastar las vacas	to graze cows
tener 50 reses	to have 50 head of cattle
la industria lechera	dairy farming
el ganado lechero	dairy herd
ordeñar las vacas	to milk cows
el ordeño	milking
la cuota para la producción de la leche	milk (production) quota
los productos lácteos	dairy produce
el mal/la enfermedad de la vaca loca	mad cow disease
el establo	cowshed

el corral	farmyard
el rebaño de ovejas/cabras	flock of sheep/goats
el pastor	shepherd
la trashumancia	**transhumance (seasonal movement of cattle to new pastures: it still happens!)**
el prado	meadow, pasture
la cría de cerdos	pig breeding
los piensos	fodder

9.2.3 La industria vinícola   The wine industry

la vid	vine
la viña/el viñedo	vineyard
la cooperative vinícola	wine cooperative
la vendimia	grape harvest
la bodega	wine-producing establishment
embotellar	to bottle
el embotellamiento	bottling
la región vinícola	wine-producing area

9.3 Vivir en el campo   Living in the country

9.3.1 Las ventajas   Advantages

respirar aire puro	to breathe pure air
disfrutar el paisaje	to enjoy the scenery
dejar atrás el bullicio de la ciudad	to leave behind the bustle of the city
aprovechar la paz y tranquilidad	to enjoy the peace and quiet
vivir en armonía con la naturaleza	to live in harmony with nature
buscarse una vida tranquila	to seek a quiet life
la gente tiene tiempo para hablar	people have time to talk
amanecer con el canto de los pájaros	**to wake up to bird song**
encontrar la casita de sus sueños en el campo	**to find one's dream cottage in the country**
aislarse en lo más hondo del campo	**to cut oneself off in the depths of the countryside**

9.3.2 Los inconvenientes

Disadvantages

la necesidad de mejorar la red de carreteras	the need to improve the road network
se llega por una carretera estrecha y tortuosa	you get to it along a narrow, winding road
lleno/a de baches	full of potholes
la falta de servicios	the lack of services
la falta de transportes públicos	lack of public transport
la supresión de las líneas de autobús/tren	closure of bus/train routes
se tarda bastante en llegar a la ciudad	it takes quite some time to get into town
vivir en un pueblo aislado	to live in a remote village
en caso de emergencia	in emergency
no estás seguro/a de que tengas la mejor atención médica	you're not sure of getting the best medical attention
los chismes del pueblo	village gossip
el 'qué dirán?'	what the neighbours will say
meter la nariz en las vidas ajenas	to poke one's nose into other people's lives
el ambiente opresivo de la vida del pueblo	the oppressive atmosphere of village life
cortar el suministro de agua/ electricidad	to cut off water/electricity supplies

9.3.3 Los cambios demográficos

Demographic changes

el éxodo rural	the rural exodus
la emigración	emigration, migration (from place of origin, not necessarily to or from abroad)
emigrar	to emigrate
los trabajadores extranjeros	foreign workforce
marcharse a América/Barcelona	to go off to America/Barcelona
la falta de trabajo y oportunidades	lack of work and opportunities
en la esperanza de ganar más fuera	in the hope of earning more elsewhere
cobrar más en el extranjero	to earn more abroad
buscarse una mejora del nivel de vida	to look for an improvement in one's standard of living
desarraigarse	to uproot oneself
ser incapaz de adaptarse	to be unable to adapt
volver al lugar de origen	to return to where you came from

diversificar	to diversify
fomentar el desarrollo del turismo	to encourage the development of tourism
incrementar la capacidad turística	to increase the tourist capacity
alquilar habitaciones	to let rooms

9.3.4 Los pasatiempos campestres

Country pursuits

la caza	hunting/shooting
cazar	to hunt/shoot (an animal)
el coto de caza	game reserve
la caza del perdiz	partridge shooting
la caza del zorro	foxhunting
los perros (de caza)	hounds
cazar el ciervo	to go stag hunting
el/la cazador(a)	huntsman/woman
el cazador furtivo	poacher
el faisán	pheasant
el jabalí	wild boar
la escopeta	shotgun
disparar a un conejo	to shoot at a rabbit
matar un conejo a tiros	to shoot a rabbit (dead)
estar en pro/a favor de la caza	to be for/in favour of hunting
los derechos de los animales	animal rights
el/la activista de derechos de animales	animal rights activist
el deporte en que se mata a un animal	blood sport
estar en contra de los deportes crueles	to be against cruel sports
abatir un ave	to shoot/bring down a bird
la perdigonada	lead shot
despedazar la presa	to tear the quarry to pieces
hay que preguntarse si la caza es cruel o no lo es	you have to ask yourself whether hunting is cruel or not
la matanza selectiva de focas	seal culling
ADDA/la Asociación para la Defensa de los Derechos de los Animales	Association for the Defence of Animal Rights

PALABRA POR PALABRA

la pesca	fishing, angling
pescar	to fish
la caña de pesca	fishing rod
el anzuelo	hook
el cebo	bait
la pesca de la trucha	trout fishing
pasar horas a orillas del río	to spend hours on the river bank
el coto de pesca	fishing reserve
el caballo	horse
la yegua	mare
la caballeriza	stable, stud, horse-breeding establishment
la equitación	horse riding
ir/montar a caballo	to ride a horse, go horse-riding
la romería	pilgrimage, procession (usually to a local shrine)
el santuario	shrine (to a local saint or the Virgin Mary)

 www.mapya.es (*and various links*)

10 Los transportes, el turismo y las vacaciones

la carretera	road
el camino	track, lane
la autopista	motorway
la autovía	dual carriageway
el ferrocarril	railway
la estación de ferrocarriles	railway station
la estación de autobuses	bus station

10.1 Las redes de transporte Transport networks

10.1.1 Los ferrocarriles Railways

La RENFE (Red Nacional de los Ferrocarriles Españoles)	Spanish Railways
FEVE (Ferrocarriles Españoles de Vía Estrecha)	company which runs Spanish narrow gauge lines
el AVE (Alta Velocidad Española) (f)	Spanish high-speed train
el transporte ferroviario	rail transport, transport by rail
la red española de ferrocarriles	the Spanish railway network
el ancho de vía (inter)nacional	the (inter)national gauge
el tren de alta velocidad	high-speed train
la locomotora de gran potencia	high-powered locomotive
una velocidad superior a 200 kilómetros por hora	a speed above 200 km per hour
el tren de largo recorrido	long-distance train
el tren de cercanías	suburban train
el transporte de mercancías	freight transport
modernizar el sistema	to modernise the system
ampliar la red del Metro	to extend the Underground network
construir nuevas líneas	to build new lines
es cuestión de rentabilidad	**it's a question of profitability**
incrementar la inversión	**to increase investment**
conseguir un mayor número de pasajeros/de mercancías en los trenes	to attract more passengers/goods to rail
tener trenes eficaces y competitivos	to have an efficient and competitive train service
atraer más comercio de las carreteras	**to attract more business from the roads**

reducir las tarifas	to reduce fares
quitar los trenes	to cut train services
eliminar las líneas no rentables	to close down unprofitable lines
el único medio de transporte público	the only means of public transport
la privatización/nacionalización de los ferrocarriles	privatisation/nationalisation of the railways

10.1.2 Las carreteras — Roads

la línea de autobús	bus route
mejorar el servicio de autobuses	to improve the bus service
mejorar el horario	to improve the timetable
llegar/salir a intervalos regulares	to arrive/depart at regular intervals
los autobuses siempre van atestados	the buses are always full
el abono de transportes semanal/ mensual	weekly/monthly travel card
el carril bus	bus lane
el transporte pasajero rápido	rapid passenger transport
reintroducir los tranvías eléctricos	to reintroduce electric trams
la calzada	roadway
el cruce peligroso	dangerous junction/crossroads
el punto negro	(accident) black spot
la velocidad excesiva	excessive speed
el MOPU (Ministerio de Obras Públicas)	Ministry of Transport
la infraestructura	infrastructure
la seguridad	safety
la carretera de peaje	toll road
el desplazamiento	movement (from one place to another)
desplazarse	to travel, move about
el tráfico de largo recorrido	long-distance traffic
el volumen de tráfico	volume of traffic
planificar la red de carreteras	to plan the road network
el programa de construcción de carreteras	road building programme
el factor más importante en la planificación de las carreteras	the most important factor in road planning
abrir un nuevo tramo	to open a new section (of road)
evitar daño medioambiental	to avoid environmental damage
cometer un atropello ecológico	to commit an ecological outrage
el coste medioambiental	the environmental cost
incrementar los impuestos sobre la gasolina	to increase tax on petrol
la falta de dinero para pagar la infraestructura	the lack of money to pay for the infrastructure

10.1.3 Los transportes aéreos — Air transport

la línea aérea	airline
la línea aérea de bajo precio	low-cost/budget airline
el vuelo chárter	charter flight
el vuelo regular	scheduled flight
la seguridad aérea	air safety, safety in the air
el registro de equipaje	baggage search
facturar el equipaje	to check in
la franquicia de equipaje	baggage allowance
radiografiar	to X-ray
el jumbo	jumbo jet
el retraso	delay
el desfase	jet lag
la diferencia de horario	time difference
emitir x toneladas de dióxido de carbono	to emit x tons of carbon dioxide
estrellarse con la pérdida de 300 vidas	to crash with the loss of 300 lives
el siniestro	disaster
la catástrofe	catastrophe, disaster
el fallo mecánico	mechanical fault
desplomarse del cielo	**to fall out of the sky**
atribuirse a un fallo humano	**to be attributed to human error**

10.1.4 Los transportes por agua — Water transport

se tarda más	it takes longer
el ferry	(car) ferry
el muelle	quay
la hidroala	hydrofoil
el aerodeslizador	**hovercraft**
el petrolero	**oil tanker**
el transatlántico	**liner**
el buque de carga	**freighter**
el buque salvavidas	**lifeboat**
los canales del interior	inland waterways
el Canal de la Mancha	English Channel
el Golfo de Vizcaya	Bay of Biscay
el (Mar) Mediterráneo	Mediterranean (Sea)
el Estrecho de Gibraltar	Strait of Gibraltar
la travesía	crossing
hacer un crucero	to go on a cruise
marearse	**to get seasick**
naufragar	**to be shipwrecked**
ahogarse	**to be drowned**
hundirse	**to sink**

el rescate marítimo	sea rescue
el puesto de guardacostas	coastguard station

10.1.5 El transporte particular — Private transport

el permiso de conducir	driving licence
el código de la circulación	Highway Code
el aparcamiento para turismos	parking for private cars
el aparcamiento subterráneo	underground car park
el parquímetro	parking meter
la multa de aparcamiento	parking ticket/fine
acelerar la marcha	to step on the accelerator, put one's foot down
adelantar	to overtake
la velocidad máxima	maximum speed
¡a más de 50 semáforo en rojo!	if you do more than 50kph the light will turn red! (traffic calming device common in Spain)
la zona de velocidad controlada por radar	speed trap area
los detectores automáticos de velocidad	speed cameras/clocks
ponerle una multa a alguien en el acto	to fine somebody on the spot
las cámaras en carretera	speed cameras
te quitan tres puntos en tu permiso de conducir	you collect three points on your driving licence
atropellar	to knock over, run over
tener un encontronazo	to have a collision
estrellarse contra	to crash into
chocar de frente	to crash head-on
patinar	to skid
el/la lesionado/a	casualty
tener una avería	to break down
estar averiado	to be broken down
hacer autostop/ir en autostop	to hitch-hike
el/la autostopista	hitch-hiker
compartir el coche	to 'car-share'
ofrecer llevarle a alguien	to offer someone a lift
prescindir del coche	to do without the car
dejar el coche en el garaje	to leave the car in the garage
un coche de alto consumo de gasolina	'gas guzzler'
incrementar el impuesto sobre el combustible	to increase the duty on fuel

You will find further vocabulary on town traffic in Chapter 8.

10.2 El turismo   Tourism

10.2.1 La industria turística   The tourist industry

el tour operador	tour operator
el paquete	package
el viaje con todo incluido	package tour
las zonas costeras	the coastal areas
las playas están a rebosar	**the beaches are overflowing**
los excursionistas	day-trippers
la localización geográfica	geographical situation
España está a tope de turistas	Spain is bursting with tourists
las previsiones para este año	the forecast for this year
se espera recibir a cuarenta millones de visitantes	forty million visitors are expected
estar a dos horas de vuelo de Londres	to be two hours' flight from London
llegar en el ferry desde Plymouth	to arrive on the Plymouth ferry
España es un país turísticamente muy organizado	Spain is a well-organised tourist destination
la relación precio-calidad	the price-quality ratio
el turismo de masas	mass tourism
el turismo de calidad	quality tourism
el turismo alternativo	alternative tourism
desarrollar el interior	to develop inland areas
dirigirse tierra adentro	**to go inland**
una ciudad monumental	a historic town
para el turista perspicaz	for the discerning tourist
un centro turístico de primera categoría	a first-class tourist centre
la industria hotelera	hotel industry
la estacionalidad	**seasonal variation (of demand)**
la infrautilización de la capacidad hotelera	**the under-use of hotel accommodation/capacity**
no se puede encontrar ni hotel ni apartamento	you can't find a hotel or an apartment
el coste del alojamiento	cost of accommodation
la doble reserva	double booking
el libro de reclamaciones	complaints book
formular una reclamación	to lodge/make a complaint
una habitación con vistas al mar	a room with a sea view
la habitación da a un solar	the room looks on to a building site
el gamberrismo	loutishness, yobbishness
las invasiones de gamberros extranjeros	invasion of foreign yobs

10.2.2 Las vacaciones   Holidays

olvidar la rutina diaria	to forget the daily routine
descansar del ajetreo cotidiano	**to relax from the daily grind**
el crucero	cruise
para todos los gustos	for all tastes
disfrutar de unas buenas vacaciones	to enjoy a good holiday
a un precio	at a price
costearse unas vacaciones	**to afford a holiday**
al alcance de cualquiera	**within anyone's reach**
no supone un gran desembolso	**it doesn't involve a large outlay**
desembolsar importantes sumas de dinero	**to spend considerable sums of money**
gastarse un dineral	**to spend a small fortune**
tomar el sol en la playa	to sunbathe on the beach
broncearse	to get a suntan
estar a sus anchas	to be at one's ease
escoger un sitio marchoso	**to choose a trendy place**
la movida nocturna	the night life
pasarlo bomba	to have a whale of a time
buscarse unos días de paz y tranquilidad	to seek a few days' peace and quiet
un sitio alejado del ruido de las ciudades	a place far from the city noise
nada más relajante que...	nothing more relaxing than...
el ecoturismo	ecotourism

www.dgt.es
www.fomento.es
www.iberia.com
www.feve.es
www.renfe.es

11 Los medios

11.1.1 El sistema y los aparatos

The system and equipment

la televisión	television (the medium)
el televisor	television (the set)
la tele	TV, telly
poner/quitar la tele	to turn the telly on/off
la televisión/radio digital	digital television/radio
el receptor	receiver
el transistor	transistor
el/la oyente	listener
el programa	programme
la programación	programme times
el canal } la cadena }	channel
una gama amplia de canales	a wide range of channels
el espacio	(programme) slot
el monopolio público	public monopoly
el monopolio oficial televisivo	the official television monopoly
la empresa privada	private company
el/la telespectador(a)	viewer, television watcher
la pantalla chica	the small screen
la 'caja tonta'	'goggle box'
el mando a distancia	remote control
la televisión por cable	cable television
la televisión por satélite	satellite television
la (antena) parabólica	satellite dish
la emisora	broadcasting station, transmitter

11.1.2 El contenido   Programme content

una gama de programas	a range of programmes
las actualidades	current affairs
el telediario	TV news programme
las noticias	news (i.e. contents)
los anuncios	advertisements
la telenovela	soap opera
el dibujo animado	cartoon
el concurso	competition
el/la concursante	competitor
repetir por enésima vez	**to repeat for the umpteenth time**
el influjo sobre los valores morales	the influence on moral values
una gran ayuda educativa	a great educational aid
ejercer control sobre la selección de los programas	to exercise control over the choice of programmes
dosificar el tiempo ante el televisor	**to measure/ration time spent in front of the TV**
adaptar su propio horario al de la tele	to adapt one's own timetable to the TV
avivar la imaginación	**to sharpen the imagination**
proporcionar cultura	to propagate culture
producir un efecto hipnótico	**to have a hypnotic effect**
una fuerza social destructora	**a destructive social force**
la violencia televisiva	television violence
producir la pérdida de capacidad creativa	**to bring about a loss of creativity**
coartar la agilidad mental	**to stultify mental agility**
perjudicar el desarrollo del niño	**to prejudice a child's development**
el vídeo	video (all senses)
el DVD (dé-uve-dé)	DVD
la película de vídeo	videofilm
grabar en vídeo/DVD	to record on video/DVD
el videocasete	video cassette
la videograbadora	video recorder
el videofilm/DVD de terror	video/DVD nasty
la pornografía	pornography
la porno	porn
el vídeo porno	porn video
pornográfico/a	pornographic

11.2 La prensa   The press

el periódico	newspaper
el diario	daily paper
la revista semanal/mensual	weekly/monthly magazine
la revista deportiva/futbolística	sports/football magazine
la revista del corazón	glossy, romantic magazine (e.g. *¡Hola!*)
el 'tabloide'	tabloid
la circulación	circulation
el/la periodista	journalist
el/la reportero/a	reporter
el/la redactor(a)	editor
redactar un periódico	to edit a newspaper
el artículo de fondo	editorial article
dar una rueda de prensa	to give a press conference
defender la libertad de la prensa	to defend the freedom of the press
la censura de la época franquista	**the censorship of the Franco years**
luchar contra el censor	to fight against the censor
aparecer en las columnas del periódico	to appear in the newspaper columns
los titulares proclaman...	the headlines proclaim...
tener prejuicio contra	**to be biased against**
ser partidario/a de	**to be biased in favour of**
tener propensión a	**to be biased towards**
un juicio parcial	**biased judgement**
apoyar una opinión política	to support a political opinion
la prensa sensacionalista	gutter press
la consultora sentimental	agony aunt
el triunfo	triumph, 'scoop'
invadir la intimidad de alguien	**to invade somebody's privacy**
se meten en todos sitios con sus cámaras	**they get in everywhere with their cameras**
demandar a alguien por difamación	**to sue somebody for libel**

11.3 La publicidad   Advertising

la industria publicitaria	advertising industry
la agencia publicitaria	advertising agency
la cartelera	hoardlng
el cartel (publicitario)	(advertising) poster
el anuncio	advertisement
los pequeños anuncios	small ads
promocionar	to promote
el mensaje	message
la consignación de publicidad	advertising budget
el eslogan publicitario	advertising slogan
llamativo/a	appealing, eye-catching
la propaganda de buzón	junk mail
el mercado objetivo	target market
hacer impacto (en)	to make an impact (on)
manipular	to manipulate
persuadir (a)	to persuade (to)
tentar (a)	to tempt (to)
llamar a nuestros instintos más bajos	**to appeal to our baser instincts**
el lavado de cerebro	**brainwashing**
obrar en el subconsciente de alguien	**to work on sb's subconscious**
subconscientemente	subconsciously
una persona de voluntad débil	a weak-willed person
el/la consumidor(a)	consumer
la sociedad consumista	consumer society
el poder adquisitivo	purchasing power
codiciar	to covet
acumular deudas con la tarjeta de crédito	**to build up credit card debts**
la interrupción constante de los programas	constant interruption of programmes
la actitud sexista de los anunciantes	the sexist attitude of the advertisers
dirigirse al consumidor joven	to target the young consumer

---

www.rtve.es

Page v also contains a list of press websites.

12 La salud

12.1 La infraestructura sanitaria — Health infrastructure

la salud	health (personal)
la sanidad	health (public)
INSALUD (el Instituto Nacional de la Salud)	Spanish NHS (National Health Service)
el Ministerio de Sanidad	Ministry of Health
el ambulatorio/el centro de salud	(local) health centre
la medicina	medicine (subject)
la atención médica	medical care
el/la médico/a	doctor, GP
el/la enfermero/a	nurse
el/la dentista	dentist
el/la especialista	specialist
el/la cirujano/a	surgeon
la cirugía	surgery (operation)
la clínica	clinic
el consultorio	clinic, consulting room, surgery (in this sense)
quirúrgico/a	surgical

12.2 Las condiciones médicas y sus síntomas — Medical conditions and their symptoms

estar enfermo/a	to be ill
ser enfermo/a	to be an invalid (i.e. permanent)
caer enfermo/a (de) } enfermar (de)	to fall ill (with), go down (with)
el microbio	microbe, 'bug'
el virus	virus
la epidemia	epidemic
la pandemia	pandemic
la alergia	allergy
alérgico/a	allergic
tener alergia a	to be allergic to
el síndrome de alergia total	**total allergy syndrome**

el agotamiento	exhaustion
el estrés/la tensión	stress
estar hecho/a polvo	to feel a wreck
no poder más	to be at the end of one's tether
desvelarse	to be unable to sleep, to lie awake
el cansancio físico y mental	physical and mental tiredness
echar mano a un medicamento	to reach for the medicine
contagiarse (de)	to become infected (with), to catch
evitar contagios	to avoid infection
el trastorno	upset, trouble
el período de incubación	incubation period
pasar desapercibido/a	**to go unnoticed, undetected**
padecer una dolencia	to suffer from an illness
el/la minusválido/a	disabled person
la minusvalía	disability
tener una lesión grave	to have a serious injury
las enfermedades invernales	coughs and colds, winter illnesses
la diabetes	diabetes
(ser) diabético/a	(to be) diabetic
la pulmonía	pneumonia
el SIDA (síndrome de inmunodeficiencia adquirida)	AIDS
el VIH (virus de la inmunodeficiencia humana)	HIV
ser seropositivo/a	to be HIV positive
el sistema inmunológico	immune system
transmitir por los fluidos corporales	to transmit via body fluids
el cáncer del pulmón	lung cancer
el infarto	heart attack
las enfermedades cardíacas	heart disease
las viruelas	**smallpox**
el paludismo	**malaria**
la amigdalitis	**tonsillitis**
la bronquitis crónica	**chronic bronchitis***
la tuberculosis	tuberculosis*

* Most diseases which end in '-is' in English are identical in Spanish except for adaptation to the Spanish spelling system (e.g. bronquitis). They are always feminine.

la gripe aviar	bird 'flu
envejecer	to age
la salud mental	mental health
la enfermedad mental	mental illness
la depresión	depression
deprimirse	to become depressed
estar acomplejado/a	**to have a complex**
recibir tratamiento psiquiátrico	to undergo psychiatric treatment
el/la psiquiatra	psychiatrist
el colapso nervioso	nervous breakdown
padecer de los nervios	to suffer from one's nerves
los nervios se me disparan	**my nerves are at breaking point**
tener los nervios destrozados	**to be a nervous wreck**
suicidarse	to commit suicide
el suicidio	suicide (act)
el/la suicida	suicide (person)
la tentativa de suicidio	suicide attempt
la regla	(menstrual) period

12.3 El tratamiento y los remedios — Treatment and remedies

¡que te mejores pronto!	get well soon!
reponerse	to recover
curar	to cure
curarse	to recover, get better, be healed
la receta	prescription
se vende sólo con receta	obtainable only on prescription
recetar una droga	to prescribe a drug
el medicamento	medicine (which you take)
las contraindicaciones	**contraindications**
los efectos secundarios	**side-effects**
el somnífero	sleeping tablet
el tranquilizante	tranquilliser
el analgésico	analgesic, painkiller
hospitalizar	to hospitalise, put into hospital
pasar un rato en el hospital	to spend a while in hospital
la casa/sala de maternidad	maternity hospital/ward
la terapia	therapy
seguir un curso de fisioterapia	to follow a course of physiotherapy
el/la fisioterapeuta	physiotherapist
operarse	to have an operation
me (le) operaron el pie	I (he/she) had a foot operation
el equipo médico de urgencia	**emergency medical team**
un descongestivo nasal	**a nasal decongestant**
despejarse la nariz	**to clear one's nose**
sonarse las narices	to blow one's nose

las más avanzadas técnicas en cirugía	the most advanced surgical techniques
el tratamiento curativo	curative treatment
la anestesia general/local	general/local anaesthetic
anestesiar	to anaesthetise, give an anaesthetic to
el trasplante de hígado	liver transplant
el/la donante de órganos/riñón	organ/kidney donor
rechazar el órgano trasplantado	to reject the transplant
trasplantar	to transplant
responder al tratamiento	to respond to treatment
la hormona	hormone
la píldora	pill
el comprimido	tablet
la transfusión de sangre	blood transfusion
la farmacia	pharmacy, chemist shop
el/la farmacéutico/a	pharmacist, chemist

12.4 La medicina preventiva Preventive medicine

la educación sanitaria	health education
más vale prevenir que curar	prevention is better than cure
promocionar la salud	to promote health
estar en buena forma/condición	to be in good physical shape
mantenerse en forma física	to keep fit
la higiene	hygiene
llevar un modo de vida sano	to lead a healthy life
la necesidad del ejercicio regular	the need for regular exercise
la función vital	vital function
preocuparse por la salud	to worry about one's health
pasar una revisión médica	to have a medical examination
el chequeo	check-up
la exploración (médica)	(medical) investigation, check-up
tomarse la tensión (arterial)	to take one's (own) blood pressure
detectar a tiempo	to detect in time
atajar la aparición de enfermedades	to forestall the onset of disease
un diagnóstico precoz de determinadas dolencias	early diagnosis of certain illnesses
comprobarse el nivel del colesterol	to check one's cholesterol level

la vacuna	vaccine
vacunarse contra la fiebre del heno	to be vaccinated against hay fever
diagnosticar	to diagnose
el autodiagnóstico	self-diagnosis
autodiagnosticarse	to make a self-diagnosis
poner de manifiesto	to bring to light
tener propensión especial a un determinado mal	to be particularly susceptible to a specific complaint
los signos clínicos	the clinical signs
darse un respiro	to give oneself a break
el ritmo biológico	biological rhythm
la longevidad	life expectancy
la natalidad	birth rate
la mortalidad	death rate

12.5 El régimen   Diet

el régimen ⎱	
la dieta ⎰	diet
una dieta sana	a healthy diet
una epidemia de obesidad	an obesity epidemic
ser obeso/a	to be obese
el peso	weight
pesar demasiado	to be overweight
comer compulsivamente	to be a compulsive eater
engordar	to put on weight
engordar ocho kilos	to put on eight kilos
tener doce kilos de más	to be twelve kilos overweight
esos kilos de más	that extra weight
los 'michelines'	'spare tyres'
la materia grasa	fatty substances, fat
los ingredientes calóricos	high-calorie ingredients
una nutrición equilibrada	a balanced intake/diet
el aporte justo de calorías	**the right number of calories**
quemar las materias grasas	to burn off fat
tener una obsesión por adelgazar	**to have a slimming obsession**
adelgazar cinco kilos	to lose five kilos
quitarse dos kilos	to take off two kilos
cuidarse la línea	to watch one's figure
sentir hambre	to feel hungry
la anorexia nerviosa	anorexia nervosa
el pan integral	wholemeal bread
la fibra	fibre
la energía	energy
un alimento muy energético	a high-energy food

12.6 El tabaco y el alcohol   Tobacco and alcohol

fumar en pipa	to smoke a pipe (as opposed to cigarettes)
fumarse una pipa	to smoke a pipe (a pipeful)
dejar de fumar	to give up smoking
inhalar	to inhale
los cigarrillos con menos nicotina y alquitrán	cigarettes with reduced nicotine and tar
el tabaquismo	tobacco habit, addiction
la ley antitabaco	anti-smoking law
en caso de que te resulte imposible abandonar el cigarrillo	**in the event of your being unable to give up cigarettes**
perjudicar seriamente la salud	**to seriously affect one's health**
destrozarse los pulmones	**to wreck one's lungs**
el excesivo consumo de alcohol	excessive alcohol consumption
beber alcohol en ayunas	to drink alcohol on an empty stomach
afecta a todo el organismo	it affects the whole system
los trastornos cardiocirculatorios	cardiovascular problems
la intoxicación aguda	acute intoxication
la borrachera	drunken state, binge
la capacidad de reflejos	reflex capacity
el nivel de alcohol en la sangre	blood-alcohol level
ingerir en pequeñas dosis	to take in small doses
la resaca	hangover
someter a la prueba del alcoholímetro	to breathalyse

12.7 La droga   Drugs

el estupefaciente	narcotic
el depresor	depressant
los barbitúricos	barbiturates
la droga dura/blanda	hard/soft drug
el/la drogadicto/a el/la toxicómano/a	drug addict
la drogadicción	drug addiction
la toxicomanía galopante	accelerating drug addiction
la drogodependencia	drug dependency
el/la drogodependiente	person dependent on drugs
el/la drogodelincuente	drug-addicted criminal

la cocaína	cocaine
la 'coca'	coke, cocaine (not Coca-Cola!)
el/la cocainómano/a	cocaine addict
la heroína	heroin
el/la heroinómano/a	heroin addict
el narcotráfico	drugs traffic
el/la narcotraficante	drug trafficker
el/la camello (*coll*)	drug pusher
la marijuana	marijuana, cannabis
el chocolate	'dope', cannabis
el porro	joint, cannabis cigarette
penalizar el consumo de drogas en lugares públicos	to make the consumption of drugs in public places illegal
la legalización (parcial) de las drogas	the (partial) legalisation of drugs
legalizar	to legalise
el/la yonqui	junkie
esnifar	to sniff
el esnifamiento de disolvente	solvent abuse, glue-sniffing
la jeringuilla	syringe
inyectarse	to inject (oneself)
pincharse (*coll*)	to 'shoot up'
engancharse	**to get hooked**
estar enganchado	**to be hooked**
costearse un vicio	**to afford a vice**
drogarse	to take drugs
doparse	to take dope
probar una droga	to try (out) a drug
estar totalmente en contra de la droga	to be totally against drugs
un programa de reinserción social	**a programme of social rehabilitation**
un programa de desintoxicación	**a detoxification programme**
el síndrome de abstinencia	**withdrawal symptoms**
tener el mono	**to go 'cold turkey'**
estar rabiando por un pinchazo	**to be craving for a fix**
la dosis fatal	fatal dose

www.mujeractual.com/dietas
www.cruzroja.es

13 La guerra y la paz

13.1 El conducto de la guerra The conduct of war

declarar la guerra	to declare war
emprender la guerra	to go to war
estar en guerra	to be at war
la guerra biológica	biological warfare
la guerra fría	the cold war
la guerra de las galaxias	star wars
la guerra de nervios	war of nerves
la guerra química	chemical warfare
la guerra de trinchera	trench warfare
una guerra sangrienta	a bloody war
la lucha contra el terrorismo	fight against terrorism
cuando estalló la guerra entre...	when war broke out between...
el/la aliado/a	ally
una potencia aliada	an allied power
el ultimátum	ultimatum
provocar una crisis	to provoke a crisis
prepararse para la confrontación/	to prepare for confrontation
el enfrentamiento	
desatar una guerra	to unleash a war
atacar	to attack
el ataque	attack
la agresión armada	armed agression
invadir	to invade
la invasión	invasion
aplastar las fuerzas enemigas	to crush the enemy forces
disparar	to fire (a gun)
incapacitar	to incapacitate
lesionar	to wound, injure
ganar	to win
derrotar	to defeat
vencer	to beat
perder	to lose
el botín	booty, spoils
el/la detenido/a	detainee
el/la prisionero/a de guerra	prisoner of war
la presencia militar	military presence
las superpotencias	superpowers
una fuerza potente	a powerful force
las sanciones internacionales	international sanctions

la pérdida de vidas humanas	the loss of human life
recibir órdenes	to receive orders
la Cruz Roja	Red Cross
la amenaza nuclear	the nuclear threat
el holocausto nuclear	nuclear holocaust

13.2 Las fuerzas armadas y el material bélico — The armed forces and military equipment

la jerarquía militar	military hierarchy
la máquina de guerra	war machine
el ejército	army
las tropas	troops
el cuartel	barracks
la flota	fleet
la armada	navy
las fuerzas aéreas	air force
el portaaviones	aircraft carrier
el avión de caza	fighter plane
el bombardero	bomber
el radar	radar
las tropas aerotransportadas	airborne troops
el destructor	destroyer
la fragata	frigate
el buque de guerra	warship
el tanque	tank
el dragaminas	minesweeper
el coche blindado	armoured car
la bomba	bomb
el cohete	rocket
el obús	shell
el gas nervioso	nerve gas
las armas químicas	chemical weapons
el armamento nuclear	nuclear armament
el sistema de misiles	missile system
La Fuerza de Acción Rápida (FAR)	Rapid Action Force
las armas de destrucción masiva	weapons of mass destruction

13.3 El servicio militar — Military service

la mili (coll)	military service
la prórroga	deferment (of service)
el objector de conciencia	conscientious objector
ser considerado no apto para la mili	to be considered unsuitable for military service

el voluntario	volunteer
el recluta	recruit
el desertor	deserter
eliminar el servicio militar obligatorio	to abolish compulsory military service
hacer voluntario el servicio militar	to make military service voluntary
la disciplina resulta dura	discipline is hard
estar a favor de un ejército profesional	to favour a professional army
hacer todo lo posible para evitar la mili	to do everything possible to avoid call-up

13.4 La paz — Peace

mantener la paz	to keep the peace
hacer las paces (con)	to make peace (with)
en tiempo de paz	in peacetime
el pacificador	peacekeeper
las fuerzas de pacificación	peacekeeping force
el apaciguamiento	appeasement
apaciguar	to appease
firmar un tratado	to sign a treaty
abogar por un cese de hostilidades	to call for an end to hostilities
aspirar por una solución negociada	to seek a negotiated solution
en los años de la posguerra	in the post-war years
disuadir	to deter
un arma (f) disuasiva	deterrent weapon
el movimiento de paz	peace movement
el pacifismo	pacifism
ser pacifista	to be a pacifist
la manifestación pacifista	peace demonstration
hacer una campaña antimilitarista	to carry out an anti-military campaign
el alto el fuego/el cese de hostilidades	ceasefire
'dad una oportunidad a la paz'	'give peace a chance'

---

www.tema.es/guerracivilespanola
www.guerracivil.org
www.sispain.org

NB: There are many Spanish Civil War sites, some of which tend to be written from a very partisan point of view.

14 El medio ambiente

14.1.1 Problemas y soluciones en general

Problems and solutions in general

el ICONA (Instituto para la Conservación de la Naturaleza)	Spanish government nature conservation body
el entorno natural	natural surroundings/environment
la amenaza a la naturaleza	the threat to wildlife
amenazar/trastornar el equilibrio ecológico	to threaten/upset the ecological balance
modificar el ecosistema	to change the ecosystem
el deterioro ambiental	environmental damage
causar daños irreversibles	to cause irreversible damage
el deterioro del medio ambiente	abuse of the environment
la supervivencia del hombre	man's survival
un planeta moribundo	a dying planet
reducir los daños causados a...	to reduce the damage caused to...
los daños irreversibles	irreversible damage
desatender las advertencias de los científicos	to disregard the scientists' warnings
el empeoramiento de la calidad de la vida	deterioration in the quality of life

14.1.2 Motivos específicos de preocupación   Specific areas of concern

la destrucción de la capa de ozono	destruction of the ozone layer
el agujero de ozono	hole in the ozone layer
el cloroflurocarbono	chlorofluorocarbon, CFC
los hidrocarburos	hydrocarbons
el spray	spray, aerosol
el aerosol	aerosol
echar/vomitar humos	to belch out smoke
los gases contaminantes	polluting gases
las lluvias ácidas	acid rain
la destrucción de las selvas tropicales	destruction of the rain forests
la deforestación	deforestation
la desertización	desertification
el recalentamiento del planeta	global warming
el efecto invernadero	greenhouse effect
los gases invernadero	greenhouse gases
las radiaciones ultravioletas	ultraviolet radiation
el derretimiento de la capa de hielo polar	melting of the polar ice sheet
derretirse	to melt (*intrans*)
el aumento del nivel del mar	rise in sea level
con sólo dos grados de más	with only two degrees (C) more
con toda urgencia	with the utmost urgency
nos quedan veinte años para evitar una catástrofe climática	**we have 20 years left to avert a climatic disaster**
la velocidad actual del recalentamiento del planeta es insostenible	**the present rate of global warming is unsustainable**
la temperatura a la que resultará imposible frenar los cambios	the temperature at which it will be impossible to stop changes
la utilización pacífica de la energía nuclear	peaceful use of nuclear energy
reanudar la construcción de centrales nucleares	**to resume the building of nuclear power stations**
el viento y el aire no conocen fronteras	**the wind and the air know no frontiers**
alertar a la opinión pública	to alert public opinion
luchar por la supervivencia de las especies	**to fight for the survival of species**
el movimiento ecologista mundial	world ecology movement

14.2 Los recursos naturales Natural resources

los recursos energéticos	energy resources
el consumo de recursos naturales	the consumption of natural resources
el consumo de energía	energy consumption
el ahorro de energía	energy saving
conservar los recursos escasos del planeta	to conserve the planet's scarce resources
los recursos se agotan	resources are being exhausted
la pérdida de recursos valiosos	the loss of valuable resources
el despilfarro	**wastefulness, squandering**
despilfarrar	**to squander**
conservar la energía	to conserve energy
el aislamiento térmico	heat insulation
encender/apagar la calefacción	to switch the heating on/off
dejar encendidas las luces	to leave the lights on
consumir un x% de todos los recursos del mundo	**to consume x% of all the world's resources**
el uso racional de la energía disponible	**the rational use of available energy**
satisfacer las necesidades de los países industrializados	**to meet the needs of the industrialised countries**
los combustibles fósiles	fossil fuels
el petróleo	crude oil
cuando el petróleo llegue a x dólares el barril	**when oil reaches x dollars a barrel**
los países del Cercano Oriente	Middle Eastern countries
la crisis de petróleo	oil crisis
sacar de la tierra	to take out of the ground
la central térmica convencional	conventional power station
minar	to mine
los adelantos técnicos	technical advances
la mayor fuente de energía utilizable	**the greatest source of usable energy**
tomar medidas	to take measures
las reservas sin explotar	unexploited reserves
ejercer una enorme presión sobre	**to exert an enormous pressure on**
una política de conservación	a conservation policy

los recursos renovables	renewable resources
la energía eólica	wind energy
el aerogenerador	wind turbine
el parque eólico	wind farm
aprovechar la energía de las olas	to harness the energy of the waves
la central hidroeléctrica	hydroelectric power station
la hidroelectricidad	hydroelectricity
el apagón	blackout, power failure

14.3 La contaminación   Pollution

14.3.1 La tierra, el mar   Land, sea and air
y el aire

la basura	rubbish
el vertedero	rubbish tip
verter al mar	to tip into the sea
producir efectos tóxicos	to have toxic effects
contaminar	to pollute, contaminate
los contaminantes atmosféricos	atmospheric pollutants
la contaminación atmosférica transfronteriza	**cross-frontier atmospheric pollution**
la descontaminación	decontamination
descontaminar	to decontaminate
la central nuclear	nuclear power station
los residuos radioactivos	radioactive waste
los efectos nocivos	harmful effects
la nocividad de las emisiones	**the harmful nature of emissions**
sobrepasar la capacidad de absorción de la naturaleza	**to go beyond nature's ability to absorb**
estar enterado/a de la amenaza	**to be aware of the threat**
el reactor nuclear	nuclear reactor
los países nuclearizados	**countries with nuclear capacity**
satisfacer las necesidades de la sociedad consumista	**to meet the needs of the consumer society**
toneladas de bolsas de plástico	tons of plastic bags
los envases de cartón	cardboard packaging
envenenar	to poison
venenoso/a	poisonous
la mancha de petróleo	**oil slick**
limpiar los vertidos de petróleo	**to clean up oil spills**
aves marinas con su plumaje empapado de petróleo	**seabirds with their feathers saturated with oil**
el reciclaje de los desperdicios/ la basura	recycling of waste
reciclar	to recycle

14.3.2 La contaminación sonora

Noise pollution

el nivel sonoro máximo	maximum noise level
los trastornos auditivos	hearing disorders
no debería sobrepasar los 70 decibelios	it shouldn't go above 70 decibels
el desmadre sonoro	the appalling noise level
la insonorización	soundproofing
insonorizar una casa	to soundproof a house
el aislamiento acústico/térmico	sound/heat insulation

www.mma.es
www. conama.cl
www.greenpeace.org.espana
www.wwf.es

15 La pobreza y el tercer mundo

un país tercermundista	a third-world country
los países en vías de desarrollo	the developing countries
los desvalidos	the underprivileged, the helpless
los desposeídos	the deprived, the have-nots
la pobreza	poverty

15.1 Los problemas humanos Human problems

15.1.1 Las condiciones económicas y sanitarias — Economic and health conditions

empobrecerse	to become poor/impoverished
el empobrecimiento	impoverishment
la desnutrición	malnutrition
estar desnutrido/a	to be malnourished
la mortalidad infantil	infant mortality
la miseria rural	rural deprivation
el hambre (f) endémica	endemic hunger/starvation
morir de inanición/hambre	to die of starvation
la marginación	marginalisation
estar marginado/a	to be marginalised
explotar	to exploit
sentirse explotado/a	to feel exploited
la lucha por la supervivencia cotidiana	the struggle for daily survival
la apatía	apathy
ser apático/a	to be apathetic
la desesperación	despair
encontrarse en condiciones cada vez más precarias	to be in an ever more precarious situation
las enfermedades relacionadas con la pobreza	poverty-related diseases
envejecer muy pronto	to age quickly
sufrir un irreversible deterioro en su forma de ser	to suffer an irreversible decline in living conditions
ser analfabeto/a	to be illiterate
el analfabetismo	illiteracy
el ínfimo nivel de la educación	the abysmal level of education

mendigar	to beg
la desigualdad social	social inequality
obtener unos ingresos inferiores a la media de la renta per cápita	to receive an income below the per capita average
vivir por debajo del umbral de pobreza	to live below the poverty line
no llegar al final del mes	not to be able to manage until the end of the month
vivir en un estado de extrema necesidad	to live in a state of dire need
no tener recursos	to have no means/resources
depender de las limosnas	to depend on charity
robar para obtener víveres	to steal in order to obtain food
deber el alquiler	to owe the rent
desalojar	to evict
estar sin hogar	to be homeless
vivir en un cuchitril	**to live in a hovel**
las barriadas de chabolas	**shanty town**
la chabola	**shack, shanty**
el chabolismo	**the problem of the 'chabolas'**
sustentar a siete u ocho niños	to support seven or eight children
el/la huérfano/a	orphan
el orfelinato	orphanage
ser carne de estadística	**to be just a statistic**
se acabó la esperanza	**there's no more hope**

15.1.2 Mejoras y soluciones   Improvements and solutions

la ayuda económica	economic aid
la organización caritativa	charity, charitable organisation
cobijar	to shelter, to house
la autosuficiencia alimenticia	self-sufficiency in food, ability to feed oneself
vivir de la tierra	to live off the land
abandonar el campo	to leave the countryside
desplazarse a la ciudad	to move to the city
compartir (con)	to share (with)
tener una auténtica política social hacia la pobreza	**to have a real social policy towards poverty**
el estado del bienestar	**the welfare state**
detectar manifestaciones de la pobreza	**to detect signs of poverty**
patrocinar a un niño	to sponsor a child
el comercio justo	fair trade

15.2 Los problemas económicos a nivel nacional
Economic problems at a national level

el préstamo	loan
reducir/suprimir la deuda del tercer mundo	to reduce/cancel third-world debt
atajar el crecimiento en espiral de la deuda del tercer mundo	to stem the spiralling growth of third-world debt
estar agobiado por el peso de la deuda externa	to be overwhelmed by the burden of foreign debt
el hundimiento económico	economic collapse
el crecimiento económico	economic growth
el Fondo Monetario Internacional	the International Monetary Fund
malgastar el dinero	to misspend money
la corrupción	corruption
los gobiernos corrompidos	corrupt governments
sobornar/cohechar	to bribe
el soborno/el cohecho	bribe, bribery
establecer severos planes de ajuste económico	to implement stringent plans for economic adjustment
un plan de austeridad económica	an economic austerity plan
un programa anti-inflacionario	an anti-inflationary programme
la inflación galopante	galloping inflation
una inflación que pasa ya del 300%	inflation already above 300%
mantener el caos a raya	to keep chaos at bay
el Banco Mundial	the World Bank
el sistema bancario mundial	the world banking system
las riquezas naturales	natural wealth/resources
aprovechar sus propios recursos	to benefit from one's own resources

15.3 Los efectos ecológicos   Ecological effects

la desertización de la tierra	desertification of the land
la superpoblación	over-population
el agotamiento de la tierra	soil exhaustion
la sobreexplotación	over-exploitation
la sequía	drought
aridificarse	to become arid
la erosión	erosion
la deforestación	deforestation
la conservación de los bosques	conservation of forests
las zonas forestales	forested areas
la irrigación intensiva	intensive irrigation

You will find further relevant ecological vocabulary in Chapter 14.

www.unicef.es
www.cruzroja.es

16 La inmigración y el racismo

16.1 La inmigración — Immigration

inmigrar	to immigrate, i.e. to migrate *in*
el/la inmigrante	immigrant
emigrar	to emigrate, i.e. to migrate *out*
el/la emigrante	emigrant
el influjo de inmigrantes	influx of immigrants
la población inmigrante	immigrant population
el/la inmigrante 'sin papeles' } el/la inmigrante irregular }	illegal immigrant

proveniente(s) del Tercer Mundo/
   de los antiguos países comunistas/
   del Subsáhara
	coming from the Third World/
	   the former communist countries/
	   sub-Saharan Africa

la Ley de Extranjería	Immigration Law
el país anfitrión	host country
el permiso de trabajo	work permit
el permiso de residencia	residence permit
el permiso/visado de salida	exit permit/visa
la libertad de movimiento	freedom of movement (i.e. of people, goods, etc)
el centro de acogida	reception centre (for immigrants)
la mano de obra barata	cheap workforce
el empleo de baja remuneración	low-paid employment
integrarse en la sociedad	to integrate into society
el derecho a la ciudadanía	the right to citizenship
el derecho de voto	the right to vote
acelerar el proceso integrador	**to speed up the process of integration**
la concesión de la nacionalidad	the granting of nationality

tras cinco años de residencia
   continuada
	after five years' continuous
	   residence

el trabajador invitado	guest worker, immigrant worker
vivir fuera de su país de origen	to live outside one's country of origin
residir legalmente en...	to reside legally in...
la segunda generación	second generation
el matrimonio mixto	mixed marriage

solicitar/pedir asilo (político)	to seek (political) asylum
la solicitud de asilo	application for asylum
el solicitante de asilo político	asylum-seeker
la inmigración ilegal	illegal immigration
una riada creciente de inmigrantes clandestinos/ilegales	an increasing flow of illegal immigrants
agravar la escasez de viviendas	to aggravate the housing shortage
el/la refugiado/a de la persecución política	refugee from political persecution
la tortura	torture
repatriar	to repatriate

16.2 El racismo   Racism

16.2.1 La discriminación racial Racial discrimination

el brote de racismo	outburst of racism
el racismo encubierto	hidden racism
el odio racista	race hatred
la agresión	aggression
discriminar	to discriminate
las desigualdades raciales	racial inequalities
un acto humillante	a humiliating act
humillar	to humiliate
la mano dura de la policía	police heavy-handedness
negar los derechos del hombre	to deny human rights
la vulneración de derechos individuales	infringement of individual rights
pisotear los principios morales	to trample on moral principles
un ciudadano de segunda categoría	a second-class citizen

16.2.2 Las actitudes racistas Racist attitudes

la xenofobia	xenophobia
la extrema derecha	the extreme right
albergar sentimientos racistas	to harbour racist feelings
el movimiento neonazi	neo-Nazi movement
el/la judío/a	Jew
el sentimiento antijudío	anti-Jewish feeling
el antisemitismo	anti-Semitism
el choque de culturas	clash of cultures
fomentar el odio religioso	to stir up religious hatred

el ataque de carácter racista	racist attack
el atraco	mugging, hold-up
atracar	to mug, hold up
apalear	to beat up
el asesinato racista	racist murder
un incidente racista	a racist incident
un caso conocido de racismo	a known case of racism
una campaña de terror	a campaign of terror
una escalada de la violencia racista	an escalation of racist violence
una ley discriminatoria	a discriminatory law
estar/sentirse marginado/a	to be/feel marginalised
las cosas han empeorado	things have got worse
corregir una situación alarmante	to rectify an alarming situation
representar un amplio espectro social	to represent a wide spectrum of society
la incapacidad de vivir juntos	inability to live together

16.2.3 Vivir juntos   Living together

coexistir	to coexist
la minoría étnica	ethnic minority
preservar su identidad cultural	to retain one's cultural identity
el patrimonio cultural	cultural heritage
la eliminación de todas formas de racismo	elimination of all forms of racism
ser receptivo/a a la diversidad cultural	to be open to cultural diversity
las ventajas de vivir en una sociedad multirracial	the benefits of living in a multiracial society
vivir en una armonía racial	to live in racial harmony
tener respeto por la cultura de cada uno	to have respect for each other's culture

www.terra.es/racismo
www.imsersomigracion.upco.es

17 Las relaciones internacionales

17.1 La diplomacia — Diplomacy

el protocolo	protocol
la diplomacia	diplomacy
diplomático/a	diplomatic
la ONU (Organización de las Naciones Unidas)	UN (United Nations)
la Asamblea General	the General Assembly
las relaciones hispano-británicas	Anglo-Spanish relations
un acuerdo bilateral	a bilateral agreement
la política exterior	foreign policy
los intereses nacionales	national interests
la presencia extranjera	foreign presence
el Ministerio de Asuntos Exteriores	Foreign Office
el Ministerio de Defensa	Ministry of Defence
el ministro de Asuntos Exteriores	Foreign Secretary
la inversión extranjera	foreign investment
invertir	to invest
el indicador económico	economic indicator
la internacionalización de la economía	the internationalisation of the economy
la multinacional extranjera	foreign multinational (company)

17.2 La Unión Europea (UE) — The European Union (EU)

17.2.1 La organización y las instituciones — The organisation and institutions

la Unión Europea	European Union
el Tratado de Roma	Treaty of Rome
la Europa occidental	western Europe
ingresar en el antiguo Mercado Común	to join the former Common Market
solicitar la adhesión a la UE	to apply for membership of the EU
la apertura oficial de las negociaciones	the official opening of negotiations
el ingreso de España en la UE en 1986	the entry of Spain into the EU in 1986

el Pacto de Adhesión	Membership Pact
la integración en Europa	integration into Europe
las negociaciones	negotiations
negociar	to negotiate
el Parlamento Europeo	the European Parliament
el/la eurodiputado/a	member of the European Parliament (MEP)
el Consejo de Europa	Council of Europe
el Banco Europeo de Inversiones	the European Investment Bank
PIB (Producto Interior Bruto)	GNP (Gross National Product)
la competencia libre	free competition
el impuesto sobre el valor añadido (IVA)	Value Added Tax (VAT)
la política agrícola común (PAC)	common agricultural policy (CAP)
los países miembros	member countries
la unión aduanera	customs union
la homologación de instituciones	standardisation of institutions
el convenio	agreement
el/la funcionario/a	civil servant
el pasaporte comunitario	Community passport
el sistema monetario europeo (SME)	European monetary system (EMS)
una moneda común	a common currency
el estreno del euro en el 2002	the launch of the euro in 2002
la eurozona	Eurozone, Euroland
la armonización de las políticas económicas	harmonisation of economic policies
el período transitorio	transition period
el arancel	customs tariff
el desarme arancelario	removal of tariff barriers
firmar un acuerdo de cooperación	to sign a cooperation agreement
la ampliación de la UE	expansion of the EU
basta ya con los veinticinco	25's enough (relating to the EU)

17.2.2 Los efectos de la adhesión a la UE — The effects of joining the EU

hacer frente al desafío de la adhesión	to face up to the challenge of membership
el desarrollo regional	regional development
el aumento de las importaciones/ exportaciones	increase in imports/exports

la competencia europea	European competition
renunciar a una parte de su soberanía	to give up a degree of sovereignty
eliminar las barreras	to break down barriers
la libertad de la circulación de mercancías (personas, capitales)	freedom of movement of goods (people, capital)
la modernización de estructuras	modernisation of structures
modernizar	to modernise
una mayor renta agraria	a greater agricultural income
compartir las aguas pesqueras	to share fishing waters
la flota pesquera española	the Spanish fishing fleet
el desarrollo industrial	industrial development
la ampliación del mercado nacional	increasing the national market
el rendimiento exigido por la UE	performance required by the EU
la compañía exportadora/ importadora	export/import company
el incremento del coste de la vida	increase in the cost of living
protegerse del impacto del cambio	to protect oneself from the effects of change
adaptarse a la competencia comunitaria	to adapt to Community-wide competition
la subida general de precios alimenticios	general rise in food prices
el consumidor español	the Spanish consumer
un abaratamiento para el consumidor	a price cut for the consumer
ampliar sus gamas de productos	to widen one's range of products
homologar los niveles de calidad	to standardise quality levels
la supresión de barreras proteccionistas	the abolition of protectionist barriers
las barreras aduaneras	customs barriers
el movimiento de trabajadores	the movement of workers
una mayor estabilidad	a greater stability
la sobreexplotación de los recursos del mar	over-exploitation of the sea's resources
la conservación y la gestión de los recursos	conservation and management of resources
la estrategia energética común	common energy strategy
la igualdad de oportunidades para todos los cuidadanos europeos	equality of opportunity for all European citizens
los retos para el futuro	challenges for the future
añorar la vuelta de la peseta	to long for the return of the peseta
ser euroescéptico/a	to be (a) Eurosceptic

17.3 La OTAN — NATO

la Organización del Tratado del Atlántico del Norte	North Atlantic Treaty Organisation
el secretario general	general secretary
permanecer en la Alianza Atlántica	to remain in the Atlantic Alliance
integrarse en la estructura militar de mando	to become part of the military command structure
la situación de seguridad	the security situation
los aliados	the allies
la defensa de Europa	the defence of Europe
la pérdida de la libertad de acción	loss of freedom of action
los objetivos militares	military objectives
el Pacto de Varsovia	Warsaw Pact
en la época de la guerra fría	at the time of the Cold War
la carrera de armamentos	the arms race
los países no alineados	the non-aligned countries
el valor estratégico de España	Spain's strategic value
la importancia militar	military importance
supeditar la libertad de acción a la OTAN	to subordinate freedom of action to NATO
firmar un acuerdo mutuo de defensa	to sign a mutual defence agreement
deshacerse de las bases norteamericanas	to get rid of American bases
la presencia militar	military presence
la cumbre	summit (meeting)
el equilibrio militar	military balance
el desequilibrio	imbalance
el presupuesto defensivo	the defence budget

17.4 Gibraltar — Gibraltar

el Peñón/la Roca	the Rock (i.e. Gibraltar)
gibraltareño/a	Gibraltarian
el/la llanito/a (coll)	Gibraltarian
el contencioso de Gibraltar	the argument over Gibraltar

la colonia británica	British colony
la descolonización	decolonisation
descolonizar	to decolonise
resolver el problema de Gibraltar	to solve the Gibraltar problem
abordar las cuestiones de la soberanía	to tackle the questions of sovereignty
la autodeterminación	self-determination
la devolución de Gibraltar a España	the return of Gibraltar to Spain
ceder el Peñón	to give up the Rock
recuperar Gibraltar	to regain/get Gibraltar back
demostrar una capacidad de compromiso	to show a capacity for compromise
una soberanía compartida	shared sovereignty
las discusiones concluyeron sin acuerdo	the discussions ended without an agreement
los gibraltareños no quieren someterse a la soberanía española	the Gibraltarians don't want to submit to Spanish rule
a través de los canales diplomáticos ordinarios	through normal diplomatic channels
la importancia estratégica	strategic importance
la seguridad del Estrecho	the security of the Strait
el paraíso fiscal	tax haven
considerar los aspectos militares y estratégicos	to consider the military and strategic aspects
levantar restricciones	to lift restrictions
abrir la verja	to open the frontier gate (between Spain and Gibraltar)
la apertura de la verja	the opening of the frontier gate (between Spain and Gibraltar)
la frontera terrestre	the land frontier
los aduaneros españoles se ponen en paro técnico	the Spanish Customs work to rule

www.un.org/spanish
www.europarl.es
www.telemadrid.es
www.madrid.org

18 La política

18.1 La democracia — Democracy

18.1.1 El sistema parlamentario — The parliamentary system

el Parlamento	Parliament
las Cortes	(Spanish) Parliament
la Cámara	Chamber
el Congreso de los Diputados	the Congress of Deputies (Spanish lower house)
la Cámara de los Comunes	House of Commons
la Cámara de los Lores	House of Lords
el presidente del gobierno	president, prime minister
el/la primer(a) ministro/a	prime minister
el gabinete	cabinet
el partido	party
los máximos dirigentes del partido	the top party leaders
el/la líder	leader
bajo el liderazgo de Aznar	under the leadership of Aznar
el gobierno encabezado por Zapatero	the government headed by Zapatero
gobernar	to govern
un gobierno de izquierdas/derechas	a left-wing/right-wing government
derechista	right-wing (adj)
izquierdista	left-wing (adj)
el ala (f) derecha del partido	the right wing of the party
el comunismo	communism
comunista	communist
el/la comunista	communist (n)
el socialismo	socialism
socialista	socialist
el/la socialista	socialist (n)
el gobierno laborista	Labour government
el partido centrista	centre party
el conservadurismo	conservatism
conservador/a	conservative
el/la conservador/a	conservative (n)
el poder político	political power
el grupo político	political group
la agrupación política	political grouping
el/la politico/a	politician

la política	politics/policy
la política verde	green politics
la clase media alta/baja	the upper/lower middle class
con el apoyo de la clase obrera	with working-class support
apoyar	to support
el debate	debate
el discurso	speech
la réplica	reply
la polémica	discussion, argument, polemic
por motivos políticos	for political motives/reasons
la oposición	the opposition
la actitud política	political attitude
mantener las fuerzas de orden público	to maintain the forces of public order
lograr el objetivo de sacar a España adelante	to achieve the objective of moving Spain forward
los derechos humanos	human rights
salvaguardar las libertades y los derechos del pueblo	to safeguard the freedoms and rights of the people
mantener vivo el sistema democrático	to keep the democratic system alive

18.1.2 Las elecciones   Elections

elegir	to elect
las elecciones generales	general election
las elecciones autonómicas	regional government/ *autonomía* elections
la campaña electoral	election campaign
el electorado	**electorate**
ganar 100 escaños	to win 100 (parliamentary) seats
el voto	vote
votar (por los socialistas)	to vote (for the socialists)
las urnas	ballot boxes
acudir a las urnas	to go to the polls
el referéndum	referendum
el/la portavoz	spokesperson
el sondeo	opinion poll
el boicot	boycott
boicotear	to boycott

18.2 La dictadura — Dictatorship

el régimen	regime
el franquismo	Francoism, politics of the Franco regime
en la época franquista	in Franco's time
el dictador	dictator
la dictadura	dictatorship
el Caudillo	fascist leader (esp with reference to Franco)
el fascismo	fascism
fascista	fascist (*adj*)
el/la fascista	fascist (*n*)
el/la facha	derogatory slang term for fascist
ultraderechista	extreme right-wing
el golpe de estado	*coup d'état*
el golpismo	coup mentality
el/la golpista	one who takes part in a coup
el gobierno títere	puppet government

18.3 La violencia política — Political violence

18.3.1 Los responsables — The perpetrators

el/la terrorista	terrorist
la organización terrorista	terrorist organisation
el grupo terrorista	terrorist group
el/la guerrillero/a	guerrilla
la guerra de guerrillas	guerrilla warfare
los rebeldes	the rebels
el/la simpatizante	sympathiser
el grupo separatista	separatist group
ETA (Euskadi Ta Askatasuna)	ETA (Basque separatist group)
etarra	member of, or to do with, ETA
una célula del Al-Quaeda	an Al-Quaeda cell

18.3.2 Sus razones y objectivos — Their reasons and objectives

derrocar el gobierno	to bring down the government
la corrupción de los políticos	political corruption
corromper	to corrupt
corrompido/a	corrupt
la ley del patrón	the law of the rich owner/boss
luchar por la independencia	to struggle/fight for independence

18.3.3 Sus métodos

Their methods

protestar	to protest
la sublevación	uprising
la revolución	revolution
revolucionario/a	revolutionary
los disturbios callejeros	street riots
el cuartelazo	military uprising, army coup
el golpe militar	military coup
las operaciones guerrilleras	guerrilla operations
la violencia terrorista	terrorist violence
el atentado terrorista	terrorist outrage
el atentado con bomba	bomb outrage
secuestrar	to kidnap
el coche bomba	car bomb
el hombre/la mujer bomba	suicide bomber
entregar su vida (por)	to give up one's life (for)
la bomba de relojería	booby-trap bomb
el explosivo Semtex	Semtex explosive
volar un tren	to blow up a train
asesinar	to murder
el asesinato	murder
quitarle la vida a alguien	to take someone's life
mutilar	to maim
lesionar	to injure
herir	to wound
degollar a alguien	to behead sb/cut sb's throat
rescatar	to ransom
el rescate	ransom
el atentado	outrage/attempt on someone's life
el asesinato político	political assassination/murder
hundir el país en la guerra civil	to plunge the country into civil war
las matanzas colectivas	mass killings
la masacre sangrienta	bloody massacre
ahogar(se) en sangre	to drown in blood
matar por matar	to kill for the sake of killing
crear continuos conflictos	to create continual conflicts
la canción de protesta	protest song
'el pueblo unido jamás será vencido'	'the people united will never be defeated'
el alto el fuego	cease-fire

18.3.4 Sus víctimas — Their victims

el/la victima	victim
la desaparición	disappearance
tomar a una persona como rehén	to take someone hostage
los rehenes detenidos en Iraq	the hostages held in Iraq
estar sobrecogido/a por el terror	to be cowed by terror
los desaparecidos violentamente	those who have disappeared by force

18.3.5 Las contramedidas — Counter-measures

los organismos internacionales de derechos humanos	international human rights organisations
evitar una guerra civil	to avoid a civil war
firmar una tregua	to sign a truce
romper una tregua	to break a truce
la ruptura de una tregua	the breaking of a truce
desactivar una bomba	to defuse a bomb
el artificiero/experto en desactivar explosivos	bomb disposal expert
tener el apoyo del gobierno	to have the support of the government

18.4 La monarquía — The monarchy

18.4.1 La Familia Real — The Royal Family

el/la monarca	monarch
el/la soberano/a	sovereign
los Reyes de España	King and Queen of Spain
el Príncipe de Asturias	Prince of Asturias
la Infanta Elena	Princess Elena
la corona española	the Spanish crown
la Familia Real	Royal Family
la Zarzuela	home of Spanish royal family
el presupuesto anual	annual budget
el Jefe del Estado	Head of State
la coronación	coronation
las obligaciones oficiales	official duties
reinar	to reign
el reino	kingdom, realm
durante el reinado de	during the reign of

la Constitución de 1978	the 1978 Constitution
el sistema constitucional	constitutional system
el jefe de las Fuerzas Armadas	chief of the armed forces
mantenerse por encima de la política cotidiana	to remain above everyday politics
cumplir con su deber	to fulfil one's duty
las cuestiones protocolarias	matters of protocol
tener sangre real	to have royal blood

18.4.2 En pro y en contra de la monarquía — For and against the monarchy

ser monárquico/a	to be a monarchist
desde un punto de vista (anti-) monárquico...	from a(n anti-)monarchist point of view
estar en pro/en contra de la monarquía	to be for/against the monarchy
gozar del privilegio	to enjoy privilege
privilegiado/a	privileged
gozar del poder hereditario	to enjoy hereditary power
disfrutar de la riqueza heredada	to enjoy inherited (unearned) wealth
deberían trabajar como cualquier hijo/a de vecino	they should have to work like any other citizen
pagar los impuestos	to pay taxes
ofrecer estabilidad	to offer stability
gozar de un prestigio sin parangón	to enjoy unequalled prestige
hacerse querer por todos	to be loved by all
el Rey Juan Carlos ...	King Juan Carlos ...
... fue el protagonista de la transición democrática	... was the leader of the transition to democracy
... jugó un papel primordial en el cambio hacia la democracia	... played a fundamental role in the change to democracy

18.5 Las autonomías   The self-governing regions

el gobierno regional	regional government
el deseo autonómico	desire for regional government
el autogobierno	self-government
la Comunidad Autónoma	self-governing region (of Spain)
reconocer el derecho a la autonomía	to recognise the right to self-government
tener una lengua propia	to have one's own language
suscitar expectativas	to awaken expectations
esto no supone una panacea para...	this does not imply a panacea for...
crear conflictos sociales	to create social conflict
crear más burocracia	to create more bureaucracy
se tiende a una Europa sin fronteras	there is a tendency to a Europe without frontiers
la lengua catalana	the Catalan language
la Generalitat	**Catalan Parliament**
los vascos	the Basques
el País Vasco ⎱ **Euskadi** ⎰	the Basque Country
el euskera	Basque (language)

www.casareal.es
www.ac-grenoble.fr/espagnol/libreta/autonomias/portales/htm
www.elpais.es/diario/autonomias.html
www.worldbank.org

The main political parties:
www.psoe.es
www.pp.es
www.izquierda-unida.es

You can easily find other parties via a search engine.

19 La economía y los negocios

19.1.1 A nivel gubernamental At government level

la economía dirigida	planned economy
la economía del mercado	market economy
el centro bancario y financiero mundial	world banking and financial centre
el sector público	public sector
el sector privado	private sector
privatizar	to privatise
la privatización	privatisation
fomentar el capital privado	to encourage private capital
nacionalizar	to nationalise
la nacionalización	nationalisation
globalizar	to globalise
la globalización	globalisation
Hacienda	Treasury, Exchequer
el Ministro de Hacienda	Chancellor of the Exchequer
la deuda nacional	national debt
la balanza de pagos	balance of payments
subvencionar	to subsidise
la subvención	subsidy
las actividades económicas	economic activities
el despegue de le economía española	the lift-off of the Spanish economy
el mercado de cambio de monedas	foreign exchange market
tras años de estancamiento	after years of stagnation
el presupuesto	budget
el/la consumidor(a)	consumer
la tasa de cambio	exchange rate
la devaluación	devaluation
devaluar/revaluar el peso argentino	to devalue/revalue the Argentinian peso
las divisas extranjeras	foreign exchange, currency
la estadística	statistic(s)

bruto/a	gross
neto/a	net
combatir la inflación	to combat inflation
la tasa de la inflación	inflation rate
la espiral inflacionista	the spiral of inflation
invertir capital en España	to invest capital in Spain
la inversión	investment
la libre competencia	free competition
el mercado libre	free market
estar sujeto/a a las fuerzas del mercado	to be subject to market forces
Note:	
l<u>a</u> banc<u>a</u>	the banks (collectively), banking
<u>el</u> banc<u>o</u>	bank (building or company)
los movimientos bancarios	bank movements
la fluctuación de los tipos de interés	interest rate fluctuation
un alza (f) en los tipos de interés	a rise in interest rates
simplificar los trámites aduaneros	to simplify customs formalities

19.1.2 A nivel personal   On a personal level

el consumismo	consumerism
la sociedad consumista	the consumer society
los bienes de consumo	consumer goods
el poder adquisitivo	purchasing power
la cesta de la compra	shopping basket
el ahorro	savings
la Caja de Ahorros	savings bank
ahorrar	to save
la Bolsa	Stock Exchange
el/la agente de Bolsa	stockbroker
las acciones	shares
el/la accionista	shareholder
el préstamo	loan
prestar	to lend
la hipoteca	mortgage
hipotecar	to mortgage
el impuesto sobre la renta	income tax
el impuesto sobre el valor añadido (IVA)	value added tax (VAT)
la plusvalía	appreciation, capital gains tax
la tarjeta de crédito	credit card
el cajero automático	automatic cash dispenser
pedir el saldo	to ask for a balance statement
la suplantación de la identidad	identity theft
el fraude de las tarjetas de crédito	credit card fraud

19.2 Los negocios   Business

la empresa	firm, company
la (empresa) subsidiaria	subsidiary, branch
la entidad	company, organisation
los recursos	resources
el beneficio	profit
el margen de beneficio	profit margin
un negocio rentable	a profitable business
la renta	income, revenue
la rentabilidad	**profitability**
la contabilidad	**accounting**
el/la contable	**accountant**
el acreedor	**creditor**
la cooperativa	**cooperative**
el convenio	**agreement, accord**
la venta al detalle/al por menor	**retail sale**
la venta al por mayor	**wholesale**
el contrato multimillonario	**multimillion contract**
las posibilidades de desarrollo	**development possibilities**
incrementar la productividad	**to increase productivity**
mantener la liquidez	**to maintain liquidity, solvency**
las cifras de exportación	**export figures**
la importación	**import**
financiar un proyecto	**to finance a project**
la fusión de dos empresas	**merger of two companies**
el pago	payment
las pérdidas	losses
la mercancía	goods, merchandise
la planificación	planning
planificar	to plan
el riesgo	risk
arriesgar	to risk
la venta a plazos	sale by instalments

You will find further associated vocabulary in Chapter 6.

www.bancomundial.org
www.bde.es
www.meh.es
www.infobolsa.es

20 La religión

el cristianismo	Christianity
ser cristiano/a	to be a Christian
Dios	God
Jesús/Jesucristo	Jesus/Jesus Christ
el Padre, el Hijo y el Espíritu Santo	Father, Son and Holy Ghost
la Virgen María	the Virgin Mary
la (Santa) Biblia	the (Holy) Bible
el evangelio	the gospel
el catolicismo	Catholicism
la iglesia católica	the Catholic Church
el protestantismo	Protestantism
ser protestante	to be a Protestant
el Islam	Islam
el/la musulmán/musulmana	Muslim
Alá	Allah
el profeta Mahoma	the prophet Mohammed
la mezquita	mosque
el Corán	Koran
el judaísmo	Judaism
(el/la) judío/a	Jew, Jewish
sionista	Zionist (adj)
el/la sionist	Zionist (n)
el sinagoga	synagogue
el hinduismo	Hinduism
el budismo	Buddhism
Buda	Buddha
la deidad	deity
la diosa	goddess

20.2 Las jerarquías religiosas   Religious hierarchies

el Papa	the Pope
el arzobispo de Toledo	the Archbishop of Toledo
el obispo de Sevilla	the Bishop of Seville
el cura } el sacerdote	priest
el párroco	parish priest
la parroquia	parish, parish church

el/la santo/a	saint
el ayatolá	ayatollah
el imán	imam
el mullah	mullah
el rabí	rabbi

20.3 La doctrina religiosa   Religious doctrine

crucificar	to crucify
la crucifixión	crucifixion
el crucifijo	crucifix
la ortodoxia religiosa	religious orthodoxy
la virginidad	virginity
el nacimiento sin mancha	virgin birth
la resurrección	resurrection
el cielo	heaven
el paraíso	paradise
el ángel	angel
el infierno	hell
el milagro	miracle
el diablo	the devil
Satanás	Satan

20.4 La práctica de la religión Religious practice

el oficio	service
el culto	worship
rezar	to pray
las oraciones	prayers
bautizar a un niño	to christen/baptise a child
casarse por la iglesia	to get married in church
ir a misa	to go to mass
la primera comunión	first communion
la confirmación	confirmation
ayunar	to fast
el ramadán	Ramadan
el sábado (*Jewish*), el domingo (*Christian*)	Sabbath
practicar/abrazar una religión	to practise/embrace a religion
predicar	to preach

20.5 Las creencias religiosas Religious beliefs

creer en Dios	to believe in God
ser creyente	to be a believer
profesar una fe	to profess a faith
ser católico/a practicante	to be a practising Catholic
tener/sentir una vocación religiosa	to have/feel a religious vocation
dar sentido a la vida	to give meaning to life
manifestarse de acuerdo con el Papa	to come out in agreement with the Pope
sentir un vacío	to feel a gap/an emptiness
rechazar	to reject
ser escéptico/a	to be sceptical
no me hace nada la religión	religion does nothing for me
ser ateo/a	to be an atheist
el ateísmo	atheism
ser agnóstico/a	to be an agnostic
el fanatismo religioso	religious fanaticism, bigotry
la (in)tolerancia religiosa	religious (in)tolerance
las matanzas sectarias	**sectarian killings**
el culto del diablo	**devil worship**
practicar el satanismo	**to practise satanism**

20.6 La muerte Death

morir	to die
fallecer	to die, pass away (*more euphemistic*)
después de morir	after death
el otro mundo	the other world, next world
irse al otro barrio	to snuff it (*coll*)
los funerales	funeral
el cementerio	cemetery
el entierro	burial
enterrar	to bury
la cremación	cremation
incinerar	to cremate
el horno crematorio	crematorium
el luto	mourning
llorar la muerte de	to mourn the death of
la necrología	obituary
el testamento	will

21 La ciencia y la tecnología

21.1.1 El ordenador   The computer

la revolución informática	information technology revolution
abrir/cerrar una ventana	to open/close a window
acceder al sistema	to log on
el acceso a la información	access to information
la clave de acceso } la contraseña	password
almacenar	to store
el almacenamiento de datos	data storage
de alto rendimiento	(of) high-performance
apagar	to switch off
el archivo	file
archivar	to save
arrastrar	to drag
la barra espaciadora	space bar
bloquearse	to crash
borrar	to delete
el chip	chip
comprobar la ortografía	to spellcheck
la conexión de redes	networking
la conexión inalámbrica	wireless connection
la copia de seguridad	back-up copy
el cursor	cursor
mover el cursor	to move the cursor
los datos	data
la base/el banco de datos	database/bank
la ley de protección de datos	data protection law
el disco compacto/CD	compact disc/CD
el disco duro	hard disk
la unidad de disco	disk drive
el disquete	floppy disk
el disquete de reserva	back-up disk
editar	to edit
eliminar	to delete
el escáner	scanner
la fuente	font
el hardware	hardware
la imagen (*pl* imágenes)	picture

la impresora	printer
encender la impresora	to switch the printer on
la impresora de inyección de tinta a color	ink-jet colour printer
el sistema de impresión inyección de burbujas	bubble jet printing system
la impresora láser	laser printer
imprimir	to print, print out
informatizar	to computerise
el joystick	joystick
el listado	printout
el menú	menu
hacer aparecer el menú	to call up the menu
el monitor	monitor
el ordenador	computer
el ordenador portátil	laptop computer
la pantalla	screen, VDU
pegar	to paste
el pirata informático	hacker
el píxel	pixel
la potencia	power
procesar	to process
el procesador de textos	word processor
programar	to program
la programación	programming
el programador/la programadora	programmer
pulsar	to press (key), click (mouse)
pulsar dos veces	to double click
al pulsar un botón	at the push of a button
el ratón	mouse
salir del sistema	to log off
el software	software
suprimir	to delete
el tabulador	tabulator
el teclado	keyboard
la tecla	key (of keyboard)
teclear	to type

21.1.2 Internet   The Internet

accederse a la red	to access the web
la arroba	@
la banda ancha	broadband
buscar	to search
el buscador el motor de búsqueda }	search engine
la búsqueda	search (i.e. the action)

el correo electrónico	email (i.e. the system)
mandar por correo electrónico	to send by email, to email
el e-mail	email (i.e. the document sent or received)
el Emilio (*coll*)	email
conectarse con	to connect/link up with
el costo de la conexión a Internet	the cost of Internet connection
descargar	to download
la dirección	address
eliminar un virus	to get rid of a virus
el enlace	link
la hoja de cálculo	spreadsheet
Internet *(usually without definite article)*	the internet
el módem	modem
navegar	to surf (i.e. the web), browse
el navegador	browser
el/la navegante ⎫ el/la internauta ⎭	(web) surfer
la página web	web page
la red	the web
el servidor	server
el spam	spam
la superautopista	superhighway
la web	the web/website

21.1.3 Los beneficios de la informática — Benefits of IT

los adelantos tecnológicos	technological advances
ahorrar tiempo y dinero	to save time and money
aprovechar los adelantos científicos	to benefit from scientific advances
asimilar las nuevas tecnologías	to assimilate the new technologies
el desarrollo científico	scientific development
desarrollar	to develop
la innovación técnica	technical innovation
nuevos recursos para los directivos	new resources for management
una sociedad evolucionada	a developed society
trabajar con más eficacia	to work more effectively
transformar la cultura humana	to transform/change human culture
transmitir e intercambiar información	to transmit and exchange information

21.2 Otros chismes tecnológicos
Other technological gadgetry

el aparato	apparatus, machine, gadget
el equipo	equipment

la alarma antirrobo	anti-theft alarm
la alarma antiincendios	fire alarm
la batidora	food mixer
la caja de control	control box
el cajero automático	automatic cash dispenser
la calculadora	calculator
la cerradura electrónica	electronic locking
los electrodomésticos	electrical appliances for the home
el detector de humo	smoke detector
activar	to set off
desactivar	deactivate
el DVD (dé-uve-dé)	DVD
el enchufe	power point
enchufar	to plug in
desenchufar	to unplug
el equipo de hi-fi	hi-fi equipment
el facsímile/fax	facsimile/fax
mandar por fax } faxear	to fax
¿puede faxeármelo?	can you fax it to me?
la fotocopia	photocopy
la fotocopiadora	photocopier
fotocopiar	to photocopy
el horno microondas	microwave oven
el lavaplatos	dishwasher
la lavadora	washing machine
el lector de CD	CD player
el magnetofón	tape recorder
grabar	to record
el MP3 (eme-pé-tres)	MP3
el sistema de navegación por satélite	satellite navigation system
el robot de cocina	food processor
la secadora	tumble-drier
el secador de pelo	hairdrier
el sintonizador digital	digital tuner
sintonizar	to tune (in)

el sistema de seguridad	security system
el teléfono inalámbrico	cordless phone
el teléfono portátil ⎫	
el móvil ⎭	mobile phone
marcar un número	to dial a number
el televisor	television set
el mando a distancia	remote control, zapper
la televisión por satélite/cable	satellite/cable television
la antena parabólica	satellite dish
la televisión/radio digital	digital television/radio
el vídeo	video, video recorder
el videograbadora	video recorder

21.3 El personal, los procesos y las sustancias

People, processes and substances

el/la científico/a	scientist
el/la tecnólogo/a	technologist
la física	physics
el/la físico/a	physicist
la química	chemistry
el/la químico/a	chemist
la zoología	zoology
el/la zoólogo/a	zoologist
investigar	to research
el/la investigador(a)	researcher
promover las investigaciones científicas	to promote scientific research
seguir una línea de investigación	to follow a line of investigation
la sustancia	substance
el elemento	element
el compuesto	compound
el proceso	process
el laboratorio	laboratory
pasar por un circuito	to pass through a circuit
el oxígeno	oxygen
el hidrógeno	hydrogen
el nitrógeno	nitrogen
el monóxido/dióxido de carbono	carbon monoxide/dioxide
el mercurio	mercury
el plomo	lead
el complejo petroquímico	petrochemical complex

21.4 La energía nuclear — Nuclear energy

radioactivo/a	radioactive
una fuga de radioactividad	a radioactive leak
el siniestro nuclear	nuclear disaster
el reactor	reactor
la explosión	explosion
explotar	to explode
una nueva generación de centrales (f) nucleares	a new generation of nuclear power stations
montar una campaña antinuclear	to mount an anti-nuclear campaign
el contador Geiger registra...	the Geiger counter registers...
alcanzar la fusión	to reach meltdown
un blanco para terroristas	a terrorist target
como consecuencia de Chernóbil	in the aftermath of Chernobyl
la energía limpia	clean energy

21.5 La exploración del espacio — Space exploration

el satélite meteorológico	meteorological satellite
la longitud de onda	wavelength
poner en órbita	to put into orbit
el transbordador espacial	space shuttle
la lanzadera espacial	space launch pad
lanzar	to launch
la nave (espacial)	(space) ship
la cápsula lunar	lunar capsule
el satélite de comunicaciones	communications satellite
la estación espacial	space station
acoplarse	to dock

See also Chapter 14.

www.mityc.es (*and various links*)
www.configurarequipos.com
www.terra.es/personal/lermon/esp/enciclo.htm (*good for computer vocabulary!*)

22 La vida cultural

el dibujo	drawing
dibujar	to draw
el diseño	design
diseñar	to design
la escultura	sculpture
esculpir	to sculpt
el/la escultor(a)	sculptor
la exposición	exhibition
la colección	collection
el arte abstracto	abstract art
el símbolo	symbol
simbolizar	to symbolise
representar	to represent
pintar	to paint
la pintura	painting
el/la pintor(a)	painter
pintoresco	picturesque
el cuadro	picture
el lienzo	canvas
el retrato	portrait
retratar	to portray, paint a portrait of
la acuarela	watercolour
la pintura al óleo	oil painting
pintar al óleo	to paint in oils
el bodegón	still life
representar	to depict
el pincel	paintbrush
la pincelada	brush stroke
el contraste de la luz y sombra	contrast of light and shadow
especializarse en la representación de la forma humana	to specialise in the depiction of the human form
no pertenece a ninguna escuela reconocida	he/she doesn't belong to any recognised school
tiene su estilo individual	he/she has his/her own individual style
el museo de bellas artes	fine arts museum
la galería	gallery
de la escuela impresionista	of the Impressionist school

113

la venta	sale
vender por una cifra elevada	to sell for a high price
el lote	lot
la subasta	auction
la puja	bid
pujar	to bid
la obra maestra	masterwork, masterpiece
el/la aficionado/a	fan, enthusiast

22.2 El cine y el teatro — Cinema and theatre

22.2.1 En general — In general

la taquilla	box office
las butacas	stalls
la localidad	seat
el/la actor/actriz	actor/actress
el rol/el papel	role
el/la protagonista	main role, protagonist
protagonizar	to play the main part/protagonist
una película/obra protagonizada por X	a film/play with X in the leading role
desempeñar un papel	to play a part/role
despertó mucho interés con su primera película/primer papel	he aroused a great deal of interest with his first film/role
a lo largo de su carrera	throughout his/her career
el estreno	first showing/performance
estrenar una película/una obra	to put on a film/play for the first time
gozar del cine/del teatro	to enjoy the cinema/theatre
explorar nuevos horizontes	to explore new horizons
la subvención gubernamental	government subsidy
patrocinar las bellas artes	to sponsor the fine arts
bajo el patrocinio de	under the sponsorship of
contar con el apoyo del Ministerio de Cultura	to rely on the support of the Ministry of Culture

22.2.2 El cine — Cinema

el film(e) (pl films or filmes) la película	film
rodar una película	to shoot a film
el largometraje	full-length film, feature film
el cortometraje	'short' (film)

la pantalla	screen
la estrella de cine	film star
el guión	script
el guionista	scriptwriter
el/la director(a)	director
el/la cineasta	film maker
doblar en castellano	to dub into Spanish
la banda sonora	sound track
los subtítulos	subtitles
la película está subtitulada en catalán	the film is subtitled in Catalan
para todos los públicos	suitable for all ages
no recomendada a menores de trece años	not suitable for under-13s
la sesión continua	continuous performance
la película en conjunto	the film as a whole
la movida madrileña	the Madrid 'scene'

22.2.3 El teatro   Theatre

la obra (de teatro)	play
poner una obra en escena	to produce a play
la puesta en escena	production
interpretar una obra	to perform/interpret a play
la interpretación	performance, interpretation
actuar	to act
la actuación	the acting
la comedia	comedy
la tragedia	tragedy
el espectáculo teatral	(theatre) show
la escena/el escenario	stage
el montaje	design, décor
la obra está ambientada en Roma	the play is set in Rome
la trama es muy enrevesada	the plot is very involved
el desenlace	outcome, dénouement
al caer el telón	when the curtain fell
aplaudir	to applaud
los aplausos	applause
silbar	to hiss, boo
ante el público	in front of the audience
el miedo al público	stage fright
el maquillaje	make-up
maquillarse	to put one's make-up on
el teatro callejero	street theatre
los títeres	puppets
la temporada	season (theatre, etc)
subvencionar el teatro	to subsidise the theatre

22.3 La literatura   Literature

la lectura	reading
el/la lector(a)	reader
el/la autor(a)	author
el/la escritor(a)	writer
el/la editor(a)	editor
la biblioteca	library
el/la bibliotecario/a	librarian
la librería	bookshop
el/la librero/a	bookseller
el libro de bolsillo	paperback
el género	genre
la novela	novel
el cuento	short story, tale
el/la cuentista	short story writer
la (auto)biografía	(auto)biography
(auto)biográfico/a	(auto)biographical
la novela policíaca	detective novel
la poesía	poetry/poem
la obra poética	poetic work
es un/a apasionado/a de la ciencia-ficción	he/she is a science-fiction addict
el estilo	style
la narración	narrative
la historia se localiza en Madrid	the story is set in Madrid
el desenlace es una verdadera sorpresa	the outcome is a real surprise
saber contar una historia	to know how to tell a story, be a good storyteller
el cuento alcanza su desenlace	the story unfolds
el/la escritor(a) de vanguardia	avant-garde writer
la casa editorial	publishing house
los derechos de autor	royalties
ser ratón de biblioteca	to be a bookworm
disfrutar de una buena lectura	to enjoy a good read
en toda su obra	in the whole of his/her work
el premio Nobel por la literatura	the Nobel Prize for literature
la tirada	edition, print run
la reproducción ilegal	illegal copying

22.4 La música — Music

la música	music
el/la músico	musician (male or female)
la sala de conciertos	concert hall
el auditorio	concert hall, auditorium
la orquesta de cámara	chamber orchestra
la orquesta filarmónica	philharmonic orchestra
el coro	choir
el/la compositor(a)	composer
componer	to compose
la partitura	score (musical)
la quinta sinfonía de Beethoven	Beethoven's fifth symphony
una gran obra sinfónica	a great symphonic work
el concierto en si bemol menor de Chaikovski	Tchaikovsky's B flat minor concerto
la ópera	opera
el aria (f) operática	operatic aria
la zarzuela	Spanish light opera
el/la cantante	singer
el/la cantaor(a)	flamenco singer (only)
el/la cantautor(a)	singer-songwriter
cantar	to sing
el/la instrumentalista	instrumentalist
el/la solista	soloist
ser clarinetista	to be a clarinettist
tocar la flauta	to play the flute
el/la director(a)	conductor
la orquesta fue dirigida por...	the orchestra was conducted by...
bajo la batuta de...	under the baton of...
el primer violín	leader, first violin
ser muy aficionado/a a Mozart	to be very fond of Mozart
tocar la música en la calle	to busk
el/la músico ambulante	busker
la música pop	pop music
el conjunto de pop	pop group
el/la rockero/a	rock singer, rock fan
el sencillo	single (disc)
el elepé	LP (long-play record)
el CD, disco compacto	CD, compact disc
descargar	to download
el concierto	gig (of pop music)

22.5 La crítica   Criticism

el/la crítico/a de teatro/cine/música	theatre/film/music critic
se publicó en	it was published in
se estrenó en	it was first shown/performed in
analizar	to analyse
citar	to quote
la citación	quotation
es un(a) película/obra/papel/personaje/ libro...	it is a ... film/play/role/character/ book

ameno/a	pleasant
chocarrero/a	scurrilous
deprimente	depressing
exigente	demanding
esotérico/a	esoteric/highbrow
enrevesado/a	involved
humorístico/a	humorous
ligero/a	light
pesado/a	tedious
salado/a	witty
satírico/a	satirical
sobresaliente	outstanding, funny

(*Remember to make the adjective agree correctly!*)

se criticó de lento/a y pesado/a	it was criticised as slow and tedious
¡dos horas de carcajadas!	two hours of laughter!
logra que el público ría de principio al fin	s/he manages to get the audience laughing from beginning to end
mantener la tensión a lo largo de toda la representación	to keep up the tension throughout the performance
es todo un espectáculo	it's quite a show
la brillante interpretación de los actores	the brilliant performance by the actors
demuestra su calidad de primer(a) actor/actriz	he/she demonstrates his/her skill as a first-rate actor/actress
el secreto del gran actor	the secret of the great actor
fue un fracaso total	it was an utter flop
fracasar	to fail, flop

al leer/ver esta escena	when I read/saw this scene
mi primera reacción fue	my first reaction was (+ *n*
(+ *n* or *inf*)	or *to*...)
me encantó la yuxtaposición	**I loved the juxtaposition**
de... y...	**of... and...**
el uso de la poesía/del baile	the use of poetry/dance
de esto se puede inferir que...	**from this we can infer that...**
está escrito en prosa	it is written in prose
tiene un estilo muy lírico	he/she has a very lyrical style

You will find further words and phrases which could be used to describe film or literary characters in Chapter 2, and further leisure activities in Chapter 7.

www.mcu.es
www.mec.es
www.terra.es/cine
www.clubcultura.com (*may require membership*)

23 Amigos algo falsos y muy falsos

Many Spanish words of almost identical appearance to their English equivalents also have much the same meaning. Some, however, although they may share one or more meanings, are used more commonly with a different sense, as in 23.1. Some other words have a totally different meaning, which could even lead you into embarrassing situations. These latter, in 23.2, are known as 'false friends'. So pay close attention to these lists!

23.1 ¡Cuidadito!   Be a bit careful!

el aborto	abortion (but can mean 'miscarriage')
abortar	to abort, have a miscarriage
absolutamente	absolutely (but often 'absolutely <u>not</u>')
en absoluto	not at all, absolutely <u>not</u>
adecuado	suitable
admirar	to surprise
agitar	to wave (arms etc)
aguardar	to wait (for)
alterar/se	to make/get upset, angry
anciano/a	(*applied to people:*) old person
anticipar/se	to bring/take place early
antiguo	ancient, but *also* former, one-time
asistir (a)	to be present at, attend (NOT to assist)
la asistencia	attendance (rather than 'assistance')
la batería	drums (in band)
bruto	coarse, rough, uncouth; gross (weight, etc)
la cacerola	saucepan
el canguro	baby-sitter
colapsar	to jam, disrupt (e.g. traffic)
el colapso	jam, blockage
la comisión	committee
la comodidad	comfort
completo	full (hotel, bus etc)
la conferencia	lecture
el cristal	pane of glass, window pane
crudo	raw, uncooked, untreated
cuestión	question (to be discussed, rather than asked)

la desgracia	misfortune, bad luck
por desgracia	unfortunately
divertir/se	to amuse/be amused
efectivamente/en efecto	in fact, indeed, actually
la época	period of time, season
el establo	cowshed
fatal	dreadful, awful, ghastly
la frase	sentence (NOT phrase)
genial	inspired, brilliant
el genio	disposition, nature; <u>bad</u> temper
ignorar	not to know, to be ignorant of
el/la infante/a	prince/princess
la memoria	memory (mechanism)
la moneda	coin; currency
la oración	prayer
particular	private
la propaganda	advertising
la ración	portion, helping (of food)
real	royal
el régimen (*NB* los regímenes)	diet
registrar	to search, inspect (baggage, etc)
regular (*adj*)	so-so (health, quality etc)
solicitar	ask for, request; apply for (job)
suceder	to happen (only 'succeed' in sense of 'come after')

23.2 ¡Mucho cuidado!　　Be very careful!

acomodar(se)	to make (oneself) comfortable
acostar(se)	to put/go to bed, lie down
actual	present (in time)
actualmente	at present, now
afrontar	to face up to
avisar	to warn
la bala	bullet
balancear(se)	to rock, sway
el balón	(large) ball, e.g. football
bizarro	brave, gallant
el campo	field, country (as opposed to town)
la carpeta	folder, portfolio
casual	chance (*adj*)
casualmente/por casualidad	by chance
la casualidad	chance, coincidence
el c(h)rismas	Christmas <u>card</u>
el collar	necklace
el compromiso	commitment, engagement; predicament
comprometerse	to commit oneself; get into a predicament
concretar(se)	to make/become more specific
el delito	crime
el disgusto	annoyance, displeasure
embarazarse	to become pregnant
embarazada	pregnant
energético (*adj*)	to do with energy, e.g. *crisis energética* (use *enérgico* for person, etc)
eventual	fortuitous, dependent upon circumstances
el éxito	success
fastidiar(se)	to annoy/get annoyed
el fastidio	annoyance
el flan	crème caramel
la gana	desire, wish
tener ganas de	to wish to, feel like (doing sth)
gentil	elegant, graceful
el gusto	pleasure, delight; taste
honesto	decent, chaste
honrado	honest, honourable
el idioma	language
jubilarse	to retire

largo	long
la letra	letter of alphabet, handwriting, words of song
loco	mad
molestar	to annoy, irritate
la molestia	annoyance, irritation
el nudo	knot
el obsequio	gift, present
la parcela	plot of land
el/la pariente/a	relative, relation
pinchar	to prick, puncture
pisar	to tread, trample
el preservativo	condom
pretender	to seek to, try to; claim
el/la profesor(a)	teacher
quitar(se)	to take away, remove, take off
el rato	(short) while
recordar	to remember
el refrán	proverb, saying
la renta	income
revolver	to stir, mix up, turn round/over
la ropa	clothes
sano	healthy
el talón	heel (of shoe); cheque, cheque stub
la tinta	ink; dye
la tormenta	storm

24 ¡Escoge la palabra correcta!

You need to take great care when selecting the Spanish equivalent of these English words.

to appear
    come into sight   **aparecer**
    seem   **parecer**

to apply
    for job   **solicitar, pedir**
    substance (to)   **aplicar (a)**

to argue
    quarrel   **reñirse**
    reason   **argüir**

to ask
    ask a question   **preguntar**
    ask sb for sth   **pedir algo a alguien**
    ask sb to do sth   **pedir a alguien que haga algo**

to become
    + *n*   **hacerse, convertirse en**
    + occupation   **hacerse, llegar a ser**
    + *adj*   **ponerse; hacerse (*implies effort*)**
    or make verb from *adj*   **independizarse**
                                (*become independent*)

both
    referring to two people or objects   **ambos/as, los/las dos**
    both...and...   **tanto...como...**

to burn
    consume or damage by fire   **quemar**
    be on fire   **arder**

to care
    look after   **cuidar**
    care/worry about   **preocuparse por, interesarse por**
    take care   **tener cuidado**

care (*n*)
    anxiety   **la inquietud**

to come   venir
    For come in/out/up/down, etc., see also under 'go'.

to drive
    drive a vehicle   **conducir**
    drive somewhere   **ir en coche**
    drive + *adj*   **volver (*e.g.* volver loco – *drive mad*)**

to enjoy
    have use/benefit of   **gozar**
      (circumstances, health, etc)
    take delight in   **gustar (*e.g.* ¿te gustó la**
                                película? – *did you enjoy the film?*)
    enjoy oneself   **divertirse**
                                      pasarlo bien

to fail
    be a flop, not succeed   **fracasar**
    crops, machinery, etc.   **fallar**
    in obligation, duty, etc.   **faltar**
    an exam   **suspender**
    fail to do sth   **dejar de hacer algo**
    (*There are numerous other idiomatic uses: check in the dictionary!*)

to get *This is a multipurpose word in English! The best tip is to find another English word which expresses the meaning of 'get' and use the Spanish equivalent.*
    obtain   **obtener, conseguir**
    receive   **recibir**
    become + *adj*   **ponerse**
    (or convert adj to v, e.g. *cansarse* – to get tired,
      mojarse – to get wet)
    go and get   **ir por**

to go   **ir**
    go/come in(to)   **entrar (en)**
    go/come out (of)   **salir (de)**
    go/come up   **subir**
    go/come down   **bajar**
    go/come across   **cruzar, atravesar**
    go/come back   **volver**
    go/come by   **pasar**

to know
know a fact, know that…	saber (que)
know how to	saber + *inf*
know/be acquainted with a person/place	conocer
NOT to know (a fact/that..)	ignorar

last
in series	último
previous (e.g. last Monday)	pasado

to leave
go off/away	irse, marcharse
train, plane, etc	salir (de)
leave (the house, work, etc)	salir (de casa, del trabajo, *etc*)
allow to remain	dejar
abandon	abandonar

to let
rent out	alquilar
permit	dejar (+ *inf* or *subj*), permitir (+ *subj*)
let sth happen	que + *pres subj*

to listen
(usually)	escuchar
to the radio, CDs, etc	oír

to love
a person	querer, amar
an activity, food, etc	encantar (*e.g.* me encanta – *I love it*)
fall in love (with)	enamorarse (de)
be in love (with)	estar enamorado/a (de)

to look
look at	mirar
look for, have a look (for)	buscar
seem	parecer
look like, resemble	parecerse a

look (*n*)
act of looking	la mirada
appearance	el aspecto
fashion	la moda, el estilo

to manage
    manage to   **conseguir, lograr +** *inf*
    a tool, etc   **manejar**
    a company   **dirigir, gestionar**

to move
    (general)   **mover (***trans***), moverse (***intrans***)**
    move house   **mudar de casa**

to order
    command   **mandar, ordenar**
    request (e.g. purchase)   **pedir, encargar**
    in restaurant   **pedir**

order (*n***)**
    for purchase or food   **el pedido**
    command   <u>la</u> **orden**
    succession, arrangement   <u>el</u> **orden**

to put
    (general)   **poner**
    place   **colocar**
    put into   **meter (en)**

quite
    completely   **totalmente, completamente**
    rather, somewhat   **bastante, algo, un poco**
    not quite   **no del todo**

to reflect
    reflect light   **reflejar**
    think   **reflexionar**

to run
    action of running   **correr**
    run an organisation, etc   **dirigir**
    in a particular direction:
        run up   **subir corriendo**
        run down   **bajar corriendo**
        run in(to)   **entrar corriendo (en)**
        run out (from)   **salir corriendo (de)**

to sit
    sit down (i.e. action)   **sentarse**
    be sitting/seated (state)   **estar sentado/a**

sorry

when you interrupt or unintentionally hurt sb	¡perdón!
to apologise emphatically, generally express regret, be sorry about	sentir, lamentar
to be (very) sorry that....	sentir (mucho) que + *subj*

to stand

stand up	levantarse
be standing (if bodily position is of importance)	estar de pie
otherwise	estar parado
tolerate, put up with	aguantar, soportar

to stop

bring/come to a halt	parar/se, detener/se
stop doing sth	dejar/terminar de hacer algo
cease (e.g. rain)	cesar
prevent sb from doing sth	impedir que alguien haga algo

to succeed

be successful	tener éxito
succeed in (doing)	conseguir/lograr + *inf*
be next in succession to	suceder a

to take

general	tomar
take hold of, catch	coger
occupy	ocupar
take sb or sth somewhere (i.e. lead, transport)	llevar
take out (from)	sacar (de)

then

next	luego, entonces
at that time	entonoos
so, in that case	pues, entonces

time

concept or duration	el tiempo
occasion	la vez
time of day	la hora
period of time	la época
short period of time	el rato
to have a good time	divertirse, pasarlo bien

to try

endeavour to	tratar de, intentar, procurar
try out, try on (i.e. test, sample)	probar

to turn (as *intrans v*)

revolve	girar
change direction	volver
turn round	volverse, dar la vuelta
turn into (become)	convertirse en, transformarse en
turn + *adj*	volverse, ponerse

to walk

action of walking	andar
to go for a walk	pasearse, dar un paseo
in a particular direction:	
walk up	subir andando
walk down	bajar andando
walk in(to)	entrar andando (en)
walk out (of)	salir andando (de)

to wipe

clean	limpiar
dry	secar, enjugar
one's nose	sonarse las narices

to work

do work	trabajar
function	funcionar

work (*n*)

job, the work you do	el trabajo
work of art	la obra
road/building works	las obras

25 Algunos verbos útiles

The following is a selection of – mainly abstract – verbs which cannot be listed under particular topic headings but are very useful in written and spoken argument.

abolish	eliminar, suprimir
accuse	acusar
get accustomed to	acostumbrarse a
achieve	conseguir
acknowledge (recognise)	reconocer
act	actuar (*in theatre*); actuar, obrar (*do sth*)
add	añadir
admit	admitir (*all senses*)
	confesar (*confess*)
advise	aconsejar
afford	costear
agree to	consentir en, quedar en
agree with	ponerse/estar de acuerdo con
allow	permitir
alter	cambiar
annoy	fastidiar, enojar
apologise	disculparse
appreciate	apreciar (*most senses*)
	valorar (*value*)
approve	aprobar
assist	ayudar
assume	asumir
assure	asegurar
attempt	intentar, probar
attract	atraer
avenge (oneself)	vengar(se)
avoid	evitar
balance	equilibrar
bear (endure)	aguantar
behave	comportarse
betray	traicionar
blame	culpar
boast	jactarse
borrow	pedir prestado
cancel	anular, cancelar, suprimir
cheat (deceive)	burlar
check	comprobar

choose	escoger, elegir
command	mandar, ordenar
compel	obligar
complain	quejarse, lamentarse
compose	componer
conclude	concluir
confess	confesar
confuse	confundir
congratulate (on)	felicitar (por)
dare (to)	atreverse a, osar
deal (with something)	tratar de
decrease, diminish	disminuir
demand	exigir, reivindicar
deny	negar
depend (on)	depender (de)
deserve	merecer
despise	despreciar
develop	desarrollar
disagree	no estar de acuerdo, oponerse (*object*)
disagree	reñir, discutir (*quarrel*)
disappoint	decepcionar
disgust	dar asco
distrust	desconfiar de, recelar
emphasise	subrayar
endure	aguantar
envy	envidiar
excuse	perdonar
fail	fracasar
favour	favorecer
fear	temer
fight (for)	luchar (por)
forbid	prohibir
foresee	prever
forget	olvidar
forgive	perdonar
frighten	asustar, dar susto a
fulfil	cumplir
govern	gobernar
grumble (about)	protestar (de)
hasten	apresurarse
hate	odiar, aborrecer
hesitate	dudar, vacilar
hinder	impedir, estorbar
imagine	imaginarse, figurarse
improve	mejorar

increase	aumentar (*trans*), aumentarse (*intrans*)
influence	influir en
intend to	pensar
interrupt	interrumpir
judge	juzgar
loathe	aborrecer
maintain	mantener
measure	medir
make a mistake (be wrong)	equivocarse
mistrust	desconfiar de, recelar
mix	mezclar
neglect	descuidar, desatender
notice	observar, notar
obey	obedecer
object to	oponerse a
offend	ofender
offer	ofrecer
omit	omitir
owe	deber
own	poseer, ser dueño de
permit	permitir
persuade to	persuadir a
possess	poseer
postpone	aplazar
prejudice	perjudicar
pretend (make believe)	fingir
prevent	impedir
profit from	aprovechar de
promise	prometer
propose	proponer
protect	proteger
prove	comprobar
provide	proveer, suministrar
quarrel	reñir
recognise	reconocer
refuse (to)	negarse (a), rehusar
regret (be sorry for)	sentir, lamentar
reject	rechazar
rely on	contar con, fiarse de
require	exigir
resemble	parecerse a
satisfy	satisfacer
scorn	desdeñar, despreciar
suit	convenir a
supply	suministrar
support	apoyar

suppose	suponer
suspect (of)	sospechar (de)
thank	agradecer
threaten (to/with)	amenazar (con + *inf or n*)
trust	fiarse de
waste (money/resources)	malgastar, despilfarrar
worry	inquietarse, preocuparse